DRAMA CLAS

The Drama Classics ser~~~~~~~~~~~~~
plays in affordable paper~~~~~~~~~~~~, actors
and theatregoers. The hallmarks of the series are accessible
introductions, uncluttered and <u>uncut</u> texts and an overall
theatrical perspective.

Given that readers may be encountering a particular play for
the first time, the introduction seeks to fill in the theatrical/
historical background and to outline the chief themes rather
than concentrate on interpretational and textual analysis.
Similarly the play-texts themselves are free of footnotes and
other interpolations: instead there is an end-glossary of
'difficult' words and phrases.

The texts of the English-language plays in the series have
been prepared taking full account of all existing scholarship.
The foreign language plays have been newly translated into a
modern English that is both actable and accurate: many of the
translators regularly have their work staged professionally.

Under the editorship of Kenneth McLeish, the Drama
Classics series is building into a first-class library of dramatic
literature representing the best of world theatre.

Series editor: **K**enneth McLeish

Associate editors:
Professor **T**revor R. Griffiths, *School of Literary and Media Studies,*
*University of N**orth London*
Simon Trussler, *Reader in Drama, Goldsmiths' College,*
*University of L**ondon*

Théâtre some twenty years before. Molière's acutely pertinent and highly successful *The School for Wives* was given later in 1662. The next year, he was granted a royal pension of 1,000 livres, and in February 1664 the King himself acted as godfather to his first child, Louis.

In 1665, Molière's company became the Troupe du Roi and the annual royal pension was raised to 6,000 livres. In the early part of 1666, Molière became seriously ill with pneumonia and had to give up acting for many months. The summer of that year saw *The Misanthrope* and *Doctor in Spite of Himself*. Then, in 1667, *Le Tartuffe*, renamed *The Imposter*, was given a public performance. 1668 saw first productions of *Amphitryon, George Dandin, The Miser*, 1669 *Monsieur de Pourceaugnac*, 1670 *The Would-be Gentleman*, 1671 *Scapin's Tricks*, 1672 *The Bluestockings. The Hupochondriac* opened on 10 February 1673, and was instantly a success. By its fourth performance, on 17th February, Molière's illness, probably tuberculosis, had become critical. He was performing the title role of Argan, the hypochondriac, and by all accounts doing so with great energy and gusto. Then, near the end of that performance, in the third interlude, the 'coronation' scene, he was taken violently and suddenly ill but managed to struggle through to the end of the performance. He was rushed back to his house in the rue de Richelieu where he died shortly after. He was buried on the 21st, in the St-Joseph cemetery, during the night – the penalty for not having made a last-minute denunciation of his actor's life in the presence of a priest.

The Hypochondriac: **What Happens in the Play**

The play's three Acts are surrounded by a prologue,

interludes and a finale in musical, balletic style. All but the finale are often omitted in performance, though the interludes between the acts (if not the prologue) are integrated with the action. Argan is a rich man obsessed with his own health. His obsession puts him in the power of quack doctors, and of his second wife Béline, who is scheming to separate him from his wealth. As the first Act opens, we see him totting up his medical bills, then arguing with his servant Toinette, who has time neither for his fantasies nor for the quacks Florid and Purgeon who sponge on him.

Argan plans to marry his daughter Angélique to a doctor, the newly qualified Thomas Lillicrap, so ensuring himself 'family' medical care for life. But she is in love with Cléante, and refuses the suggestion. Toinette supports her, but Argan sends her away and proposes to alter his will in Béline's favour. Béline protests that she doesn't want his money – and then brings in Mr Goodfellow, her lawyer, to arrange the documents.

In the second Act, Toinette introduces Cléante into the house as Angélique's new music teacher, and Cléante and Angélique improvise a song of frustrated yearning, to Argan's bafflement. Dr Lillicrap arrives with his doltish son Thomas, who makes absurdly flattering, flowery speeches to all concerned. Béline tells Argan that Angélique and Cléante are planning to elope, and Argan (after finding that this is true by questioning his younger daughter, the child Louison), falls into his chair, bewildered beyond endurance. His brother, the sensible Béralde, brings dancers to divert him, then sets about trying to make him see sense.

Act Three begins with a long scene between Argan and Béralde, discussing the merits of doctors. Apothecary Florid arrives to give Argan 'something for his bowels', and Béralde sends him packing, together with his employer Dr Purgeon. Béralde and Toinette now hatch a plan: Toinette appears, disguised as a 90-year-old doctor, and ridicules every cure Purgeon has previously prescribed. Béralde suggests that Argan test the affections of his wife and daughter by feigning death – and, predictably, Béline is revealed as heartless, Angélique as truly loving. Argan agrees to let Angélique marry Cléante, and Béralde solves the problem of his brother's obsession with medicine by arranging for him to be made a doctor himself, in the burlesque musical finale which ends the play.

The Hypochondriac: **Origins and First Production**

Molière's last play owes its particular form as well as its existence in good part to Louis XIV. A few months before it opened, the Sun King had returned to France from his Dutch campaign, and Molière's idea was to write a *comédie-ballet* – a blend of comedy, song and dance, one of the King's favourite kinds of entertainment – as part of the entertainments which would be put on to celebrate the King's safe return from the war. The prologue makes this intention clear. And the form was a well-tried one, successful in the past. All Molière's previous twelve *comédies-ballets* had received their first staging in front of a private audience of Louis XIV and his Court. What characterised this type of play, from the first one, *The Bores* of 1661, onwards, was its mix of comedy, song and dance. Molière's skill was to integrate the seemingly disparate elements into a unified entertainment, all of whose parts reflected and commented upon the others.

The plan to stage *The Hypochondriac* before the Court at Versailles was not realised, however. Ironically, the *comédie-ballet* form was the focus of bitterness between Molière and the composer, Lully. Up to this point, Lully had written the music for those plays of Molière which required it. The collaboration had started in 1664, but in 1672 Lully obtained from the King the monopoly for most of the entertainments which involved singing. He secured significant publication rights as well. Relations between Molière and Lully inevitably soured, so that the playwright had to turn to another composer, Charpentier, for the music to *The Hypochondriac*. In effect, Molière suffered a ban from the Court, where Lully was in artistic command.

Thus it was that the play received its first performance at the Palais-Royal theatre in Paris, and not at Versailles. On top of that, the opening was delayed until February 1673 apparently because some news reached Paris at the last moment of reverses suffered by Louis's army in Holland. The original prologue also was replaced by a shorter 'alternative' version, better suited to a production in the capital rather than at Court.

The Household of the Rich Bourgeois

Unlike Molière's earlier plays about medicine (*The Flying Doctor, Doctor Love, Doctor in Spite of Himself*), the focus in *The Hypochondriac* is on the patient and not the doctor. Argan is so locked into his range of imagined illnesses that his role and duties as the head of a household are seriously relegated and distorted.

Argan belongs to the upper echelons of the bourgeoisie. Both

Toinette and Béralde refer to his wealth – as indeed he does himself, when he plans his will. His medical bills paint the same picture. His monthly outlay on his medical requirements puts him way above the level of the ordinary middle class. Even apart from his wealth, Argan's social status must be high. Certain details indicate this, such as the type of chair he sits in as opposed to the sort he offers people in the room, and the way he is addressed as *seigneur* ('Your Excellence') and *monsieur* ('Sir').

After the loss of his first wife, Argan has been left with two daughters to bring up, and he has to confront the attendant problem of their dowries. This problem, as far as Angélique is concerned, should have been easily resolved. She has met and fallen for a perfectly acceptable suitor, Cléante, who, it is revealed, is an *homme d'épée*, a man carrying a sword and therefore a good deal of social status. Yet, of course, Argan turns away from the obvious and the satisfactory in his self-regarding, obsessive pursuit of physical health.

As elsewhere in Molière's work, the socially dominant figure is surrounded by spongers and parasites. Argan is preyed upon by his second wife Béline, and by assorted doctors and an apothecary. They are united in their approach to Argan, the need to reinforce his belief that he is ill. They all stand to profit from this – the doctors by obvious means, the wife by some skilful manipulation of inheritance laws. Her exposure at the end of the play means that she has to give up any rights to Argan's wealth. Indeed, he ends up wishing to divorce her.

The Medical Profession in Molière's Time

Medicine in 17th century France was controlled by the Faculty of Medicine, and was rigidly hierarchical. There were three divisions in the profession: *médecin* (doctor), *apothicaire* (apothecary) and *chirurgien-barbier* (surgeon-barber). The first two are well represented in *The Hypochondriac*, but the third, the lowest of the three, does not feature at all.

The Doctor

The education (training hardly seems the word) of the *médecin* lasted for years. As in all education, Latin was the language used. Emphasis was placed on theory, and the doctor had to learn how to argue and pronounce in fine language and high style. But none of this was underpinned by any practical knowledge, any first-hand observation. The 'first grade' would be attained when the student had reached the minimum age of twenty-five. Then, the candidate would become *bachelier* (Bachelor as in B.A.) and go on to prepare a thesis, a short Latin dissertation on a subject chosen by the candidate. Some titles, at random: 'From which part of Christ's body did water originate when, after His death, a spear was plunged into His side?'; 'Should the moon's phases be taken into account when cutting hair?'; 'Is woman more lascivious than man?'; 'Is it the pressure of blood which causes the heart to beat?'

The candidate had to undergo an oral exam of his thesis, which could last six or seven hours. If successful, he would proceed to the next phase of his studies, which in turn would be followed by more exams. On condition that he passed, the candidate would obtain his licence to practise medicine. He would now be a doctor, and his success would be crowned with elaborate ceremonial. In the 1670s, the English philosopher John Locke witnessed one such occasion in Montpellier. In his *Journal* for 18 March 1676, Locke writes about the recipe for making a doctor: the grand procession of doctors dressed in red, with black bonnets on their heads, the orchestra playing Lully, the President who takes his seat and indicates that the music should stop so that he may speak, his eulogy of his colleagues and diatribe against new-fangled ideas and theories such as the circulation of the blood, the speech the doctor-elect makes in reply, complimenting those at the top of the medical Establishment, the professors, the academy, then more music, and the crowning moment when the President puts the bonnet on the new doctor's head.

Molière copies these details faithfully in the closing interlude. Argan becomes both *bachelier* and *licencié*, that is, he becomes a fully-fledged doctor in a single operation. Dr Lillicrap (Diafoirus) is clearly a doctor of long standing. His son Thomas is a new *bachelier*. This is indicated by the fact that he has brought his thesis, the object of Toinette's derision. Incidentally, she suggests papering the walls with it probably because it would have had an allegorical picture or engraving on its front cover. Thomas also wants Angélique to witness the dissection of a woman, as a special treat. In 1667, just such a dissection had caused a widespread scandal – and Molière would have known of this event when he came to write *The Hypochondriac*.

The Apothecary

The *apothicaire* was equal to the *médecin* neither professionally, intellectually nor socially. He was considered to belong to the artisan class, related to the grocer or the salesman. To become an apothecary, it was necessary to proceed via the stages of apprentice, then *compagnon* (companion), and finally, at the age of twenty-five, after an exam taken in the Faculty of Medicine, to *maître* (master). This exam was mainly on matters of chemistry and botany, the latter, at least, studied in a practical way in the Jardin des Plantes (Botanical Gardens) which all universities possessed.

The apothecary's job was to prepare and administer medicines according to the doctor's prescription. He gave the famous *clystère* (an early form of enema-syringe) and sent out patients' bills, as in the play's opening scene. As these bills tended to be high, the apothecary would couch and disguise them in fine, convoluted language. Bargaining often occurred, with the patient trying to get the prices down.

The Surgeon-barber

The rank of *chirurgien-barbier* was the lowest in the medical hierarchy. He was the doctor's valet, who did only the tasks considered menial. So, he would bleed a patient, set fractured bones, perform dissections, etc. No surgeon-barber appears in *The Hypochondriac*, perhaps because his precise and limited work would have had no dramatic function. When Thomas says that he must be present at a dissection, it is to discuss and explain the phenomena revealed by the dissection – but as a doctor, he would not have touched the corpse, not even with a scalpel. The 'surgeon' dissects in silence, the doctor watches and pontificates in Latin.

The State of Medical Knowledge in Molière's Time

It is a truism to say that medical knowledge and beliefs in Molière's France were light years away from their present state. But the thermometer, for example, had not been invented at the time of *The Hypochondriac*, and the microscope was hardly in use. Dissection was comparatively rare: the law allowed that only executed criminals be dissected.

Doctors knew nothing of inner organs of the living body. Surgery in the modern sense was a marginal activity. Incisions would be made on visible tumours, for example, and limbs would be amputated, wounds closed, broken bones set. On the other hand, it was not the practice to open up the rib-cage or the abdomen. Thus, theories were propounded on the basis of superficial observation only, and by examining what the body expelled. Sputum, urine, excrement, all were closely scrutinised in the hope that they would indicate what was happening to the lungs, kidneys, and intestines.

Medicine at all times is vulnerable to the abuse of charlatans, and in Molière's time there were considerable numbers of itinerant quacks who managed to escape the control of the Faculty and of the police. This is one of the reasons Toinette is able to get away with her outrageous impersonation in the final act. Established doctors 'played the system' in a legitimate way. Thus Dr Lillicrap prefers to be a doctor to the general public rather than to the great and famous. Simply put, he can get away with more.

In several plays, Molière makes the medical profession the main target of his comedy. There were large numbers of gullible people around who were too readily taken in by quackery. Even the normally lucid Mme de Sévigné made great claims for the virtues of a viper broth, and she recommended it with enthusiasm to her daughter in 1685.

La Bruyère had a couple of aphorisms which seem exactly relevant: 'Those who are in good health become ill, they need people whose job it is to reassure them that they are not going to die', and 'So long as human beings go on dying, and want to go on living, the doctor will be mocked and well paid'.

Original Staging

The opening scenes of Rostand's *Cyrano de Bergerac* are set in a 17th-century theatre, and give a good idea of conditions in Molière's time. The 'theatre' was a large room, roughly the size of a tennis court. At one end was a raised stage, with an ornate flight of steps leading down to the theatre floor. The back wall of this 'stage' was hung with painted scenery. Attendants saw to the placing or removal of props and furniture, in full view of the audience. When the stage was set, the actors strode onto it, struck attitudes and began to speak. In tragedy, the poses were statuesque (often modelled on famous artworks) and the delivery was ponderous and pompous; in comedy static dialogue-scenes (like those between Argan and Angélique or Argan and Béralde) were interspersed with fast, slapstick action, as in the scene where Argan throws cushions, or his encounters with the quack doctors.

A main difference between theatre in Molière's time and today was the behaviour of the audience. The whole theatre, not just the stage, was brightly lit (by a huge central candelabrum whose hundreds of candles were ceremonially lit at the start of the performance and equally solemnly doused at the end). The audience was there to be seen, as well as to see. They talked, ate, played cards, flirted and even duelled while the play was in progress. Some stood on the theatre floor; others sat on specially-brought seats; a group of (highly vocal) amateur critics sometimes took their seats on the stage or its steps themselves. The 'quality' had private boxes on an upper level round the walls, and regarded theatre-going as a social occasion, in which watching the play was a minor distraction. When (as in *The Hypochondriac*) there was music and dancing, it overflowed from the stage to the theatre floor. Despite such chaotic conditions, we are told that Molière himself was always listened to with enjoyment – and even that his big speeches and striking pieces of business were applauded, the action stopping dead while he took a bow and sometimes gave an encore.

The Hypochondriac: Theme and Structure

Like other *comédies-ballet*, this play has the structure of a spoken text preceded by a prologue and divided by interludes using music and dance, and which appear to be distinct and separate entities. The plot (as often in Molière) is less important than the development of character (especially) and situation. The eminent Molière critic W. G. Moore said that the real theme of the play is not so much medicine as the struggle between naivety and deception – a struggle in which language is the crucial weapon. The group of deceivers (doctors, apothecary, wife) exploit the gap between words and what they supposedly mean. As Béralde says, it is not illnesses which are destroying his brother, but their names. This psychological/ philosophical truth, running through the whole

play, goes a long way towards explaining the play's energy.
It is a riot of language.

As ever in Molière, disguise and contradiction are essential
building- blocks. Doctors and apothecaries are charlatans
disguised, so too in her way is Argan's wife. Beyond them,
Toinette, Louison, Angélique and Cléante all 'disguise'
themselves temporarily to try to make some impression on
Argan. But the most interesting disguise and contradiction is
in Argan himself. He is a permanent invalid with the
constitution of an ox, a blood-drained wreck full of wild rage
and anger, a cripple who walks without his stick, a tyrannical
egotist who is an affectionate father, a hard-headed leader
who is the dupe of wife and quacks, an employer who can
do nothing to control his servant, a patient insulted and
threatened by the doctor and the apothecary whose bills
nonetheless he pays.

The conflicts, anger and frustration which are engendered by
all these layers of contradiction make for lively action: the
stage is an explosion of movement. Argan throws cushions,
doors are permanently open, with doctors, wife, offspring,
suitor, servant, lawyer entering and exiting in a constant
procession. Argan is almost hyperactive; he goes back to his
chair only when he suddenly remembers to. The dance
element in the *comédie-ballet* structure augments the picture by
adding even more movement and lightness.

In terms of structure, the original prologue (not the
alternative) is extraneous to the main action. But the first and
second interludes heighten the movement and sense of
growing chaos in the Argan household, and prepare the final
interlude, where this time Argan is central. Everything leads

up to this fantasy dénouement. The plot is resolved, and the satire of medicine reaches its highest point. This brilliant, dazzling finale is the apotheosis of the imaginary invalid, the mock-celebration of complacent naivety, madness crowned by a Faculty of Medicine, itself lost in delirium. The uneasy co-existence of fact and fantasy has been a dominant theme all through the play. The artifice of the first two interludes reinforces this unease, but the final interlude blends the two elements in one of Molière's greatest theatrical moments. Literally, poor Argan cannot recognise himself.

Language

Molière's language is not only an act of communication in this play, it is a weapon. Sometimes it has a plain, no-nonsense directness, as in the mouth of Toinette, whose aim in the face of medical mumbo-jumbo is always to call a spade a spade and a fraud a fraud. Other characters have their own styles. Argan is neurotically hyperbolic, his brother sounds like what a real doctor perhaps should be, Angélique is polite but will not be pushed around, and the various medical men border on hell-fire preachers, though Thomas has developed a conned-by-rote baroque palaver to send everyone to sleep. For a play which is so lavatorial, Molière's language steers a discreet course, avoiding the out-and-out obscene but remaining racy and punchy.

For the translator, a significant problem is the place of Latin. In the original, the jokes built on that language work wonderfully well, but of course Molière's audience would have had a sound command of it. This is scarcely the case in the contemporary English-speaking world. My solution (principally in the final interlude) has been to stick with a limited range of Latin vocabulary and expressions still generally familiar, to tag pseudo-Latin or Italian endings on to English words, and to put it in doggerel wherever appropriate.

Martin Sorrell,
Exeter, 1994

For Further Reading

There is a vast array of information of all kinds, on Molière, his life and his work. Inevitably, the majority of these are in French. One of the soundest, most helpful and readable critical editions of *Le Malade imaginaire*, is Peter H. Nurse's book in the Clarendon French Series, first published by Oxford University Press in 1965. Although the text of the play is in French, the useful introduction and notes are in English. The remarks in the first two sections above are in part drawn from this edition.

P.H. Nurse has also written well about Molière, in *Molière and the Comic Spirit* (Droz, 1991). H.T. Barnwell, *Molière: 'Le Malade imaginaire'* (Grant and Cutler, Critical Guides to French Texts, No. 12, 1982) is a succinct and lucid monograph on the present play. W. G. Moore, *Molière, a New Criticism* (O.U.P., 1949), is the leading scholarly book in English: influential, readable and essential. For a detailed study of the social background to Molière's plays, see James F. Gaines, *Social Structures in Molière's Theatre* (Ohio State University Press, 1984). The remarks above about Argan's social standing largely derive from this book.

For the reader with a reasonable command of French, as well as access to a tape-deck, there is available a supremely interesting cassette-recording of two talks, each some twenty-five minutes long, the first on medicine in the time of Molière, the second on the dynamism of *Le Malade imaginaire*. They were written and read by the late Jean-Dominique Biard of Exeter University, and are issued on one cassette, no. F7559 in the Exeter Tapes series, available from Drake Educational Associates, St Fagans Road, Fairwater, Cardiff CP5 3AE. These talks are quite outstanding, and have been used substantially in three sections of the introduction given above.

Finally, Ariane Mnouchkine and her Théâtre du Soleil in Paris have made a compelling and imaginative film about the life and death of Molière, simply entitled *Molière*. It has offended purists and scholars with its imaginative, sometimes fanciful approach, but it does give a remarkable and often moving picture of Molière's life, and of conditions in the theatre in 17th century France. This film, issued in 1986 by Proserpine Editions, is available on video-cassette. To all the critics listed here whose work has helped in the preparation of this introduction, we record our acknowledgement and sincere thanks.

Molière: Key Dates

1622   Birth of Molière. Precise date not known. Baptised
        15th January in Paris, the son of Jean Poquelin,
        merchant upholsterer.

1633?-9 Educated at Jesuit Collège de Clermont (now the
        Lycée Louis-le-Grand).

1642   After brief law studies, obtains his licence in Orléans.

1643   June, joins the recently-formed theatre company, the
        Illustre Théâtre, Paris. 1644. Adopts the name
        Molière.

1645-58 After serving prison sentence for debt, Molière and
        troupe tour provinces. Enjoy patronage of the Prince
        de Conti, 1653-57.

1655   Molière's first full-length play, *The Scatterbrain*, acted
        in Lyons.

1658   Molière and his company return to Paris. Share
        Petit-Bourbon theatre with the Italian commedia
        dell'arte players. Patronage of the King's brother,
        Philippe d'Orléans.

1659   18 November, successful production of *The Pretentious
        Ladies*.

1661   Company moves to Palais-Royal theatre. 23 June,
        successful production of *The School for Husbands*.

1662   20 February, Molière marries Armande Béjart, aged
        about 20. December, *The School for Wives*.

1663   Molière receives royal pension of 1,000 livres.

1664	May, three-act version of *Tartuffe*. This is then banned but is followed in November by the full five-act version, performed in private.
1665	February, *Don Juan* (withdrawn shortly after). Molière's company becomes the Troupe du Roi, and annual pension increased to 6,000 livres. 14 September, *Doctor Love*.
1666	January-February, Molière seriously ill. 6 June, *The Misanthrope*. 6 August, *Doctor in Spite of Himself*.
1667	Public performance of *Tartuffe*, renamed *The Imposter*, followed by further ban.
1668	13 February, *Amphitryon*. 18 July, *George Dandin*. 9 September, *The Miser*.
1669	5 February, first authorised public performance of *Tartuffe*.
1670	November, *The Would-be Gentleman*.
1671	14 May, *Scapin's Tricks*.
1672	March, *The Bluestockings*.
1673	10 February, *The Hypochondriac*. 17 February, death of Molière.

THE HYPOCHONDRIAC

Characters

ARGAN, who imagines himself ill
BÉLINE, Argan's second wife
ANGÉLIQUE, Argan's elder daughter, in love with
    Cléante
LOUISON, Argan's younger daughter
BÉRALDE, Argan's brother
CLÉANTE, in love with Angélique
TOINETTE, Argan's servant
DR LILLICRAP (Diafoirus), doctor of medicine
THOMAS LILLICRAP, (Diafoirus) his son, and would-
    be fiancé of Angélique
DR PURGEON (Purgon), Argan's personal doctor
MR FLORID (Fleurant), apothecary
MR GOODFELLOW (Bonnefoi), notary

The action takes place in Paris.

Prologue

After the victorious campaigns of our Great King, it is appropriate that anyone whose business is writing should set about either celebrating or entertaining him. This has been the aim of the play printed here; and this prologue is an attempt to sing the praises of our monarch. It serves as an introduction to the comedy of THE HYPOCHONDRIAC, *which has been written for the purpose of entertaining him and of giving him some distraction after his wonderful exploits.*

A delightful, rural setting.

Eclogue

Dance and music.

FLORA, PAN, CLIMÈNE, DAPHNÉ, TIRCIS, DORILAS, ZEPHYRS, SHEPHERDS, SHEPHERDESSES.

FLORA. Nymphs and shepherds, come away!
    Leave sheep and lambs at play.
    I've news to delight you,
    News to excite you,
    So, nymphs and shepherds, come away!

CLIMÈNE AND DAPHNÉ. Flora calls us, come away!
    Leave sheep and lambs at play.

TIRCIS AND DORILAS. Wait! Heart of stone –

TIRCIS. My love, my own –

DORILAS. I beg, I pray –

CLIMÈNE AND DAPHNÉ. Now come, now come away!

TIRCIS AND DORILAS. One little word, we beg you, say –

TIRCIS. One word, no more –

DORILAS. I beg, implore –

CLIMÈNE AND DAPHNÉ. Now come, now come away!

Dance and music. The shepherds and shepherdesses gather round
FLORA.

CLIMÈNE. Great goddess, Flora, speak –
Delight each listening ear.

DAPHNÉ. Your news we seek –

DORILAS. We shake, we ache –

ALL. We pant, we quake –

FLORA. Be quiet, then. You'll hear.
Your prayers are heard,
Each anxious word.
Let joy abound:
He's safe and sound,
King LOUIS, home. All danger's past,
And peace has broken out at last.

ALL. He's safe and sound!
Let joy abound.
All danger's past.
We've peace at last.

Shepherds and shepherdesses express their joy in dance.

FLORA. Play music, dance and sing,
    Salute this happy day.
    Let woods with joy now ring,
    All Nature, leap and play.

ALL. Salute this happy day.
    All Nature, leap and play.

FLORA. Sing now, be glad, rejoice,
    Be heard each shepherd's voice.
    Your rival songs now test.
    Step forward, improvise.
    Your monarch's glory praise,
    This happiest of days.
    We'll hear, we'll choose the best:
    His song will win the prize.

CLIMÈNE. If Tircis's song is best –

DAPHNÉ. If Dorilas wins the test –

CLIMÈNE. I'll be his for life –

DAPHNÉ. His loving wife.

TIRCIS. Expectation –

DORILAS. Agitation –

BOTH. For such a theme, with such a prize,
    Let music play! Sweet voices rise!

The orchestra plays to urge on the two shepherds. FLORA, as judge, goes to the foot of a tree centre-stage. She is accompanied by two zephyrs. The others go to the edges of the stage to watch.

TIRCIS. The melting winter snow
   Makes rushing rivers flow,
   Sweeps forests in its dance.
   But cities, dams, châteaux,
   Must yield their place and go
   When LOUIS, Sun of France,
   Begins his dread advance.

Dancing on Tircis's side to mark approval.

DORILAS. Loud thunder fill the air!
   Bright lightning split the sky!
   Black darkness gloom and glower!
   Draw back! Bow down! Despair!
   King LOUIS comes! His hour
   Is now! His praise, his power
   Bedazzles every eye.

Dancing on Dorilas's side.

TIRCIS. Our lord's great victory
   Begins all history.
   His lance! His spear! His sword!
   The trembling foreign horde!
   That fiery, glowing glance!
   Our LOUIS, Sun of France!

More dancing on Tircis's side.

DORILAS. His triumph sing, his praise!
   Salute these golden days,
   Our enemies struck dumb,
   For centuries to come.
   They run away; they hide;
   Shout out his name with pride.

More dancing on Dorilas's side.

PAN (*accompanied by six Fauns*).
Hush, shepherds, sing no more.
Lay down the rustic flute.
Join hands, bow down, implore
Apollo with his lute
To sing great LOUIS's fame,
To praise his royal name.

To hymn such great renown
With humble, mortal strain
Is flying too near the Sun:
You'll fall, you'll sink, you'll drown.
Now silence, everyone!
Let others entertain.

ALL. Give up this humble strain.
Let others entertain.

FLORA. Too much to ask,
Too great a task,
To sing such triumphs. Hear
The verdict. Both have won.
No loser, none.
You'll share the prize. No shame –
Both nobly played the game.

The two zephyrs dance holding garlands of flowers. They crown the two shepherds.

CLIMÈNE AND DAPHNÉ (*each offering their hand*).
You'll share the prize. No shame.
Both nobly played the game.

TIRCIS AND DORILAS. We share the victor's crown –

FLORA AND PAN. Sing LOUIS's great renown.

THE FOUR LOVERS. We'll serve him all we may –

FLORA AND PAN. Until your dying day.

ALL. His mighty deeds require
    We sing his peerless reign.
    We'll praise and praise you, Sire,
    In this our poor refrain.

*Dance. Fauns, shepherds, shepherdesses, join and mingle, then exit to
get ready for the Play.*

Alternative Prologue

Shepherdess's lament.

SHEPHERDESS. Doctors, you're rogues, own up, come on!
    Your so-called learning's a great big con.
    Those strings of words like macaroni
    Are indigestible. You're phoney!

    Your laxatives, your syrups, potions
    Won't find a place in my emotions.
    I'll suffer in silence, out of reach.
    You prate and lecture, rant and preach –
    It's rubbish, a con, it's a try-on.
    You'll never be a shoulder to die on!

    Some dummies believe all your rot,
    They're born every minute.
    But the dimmest, the worst of the lot
    Is on stage now. It's our play, and he's in it.

Act One

1. ARGAN.

ARGAN (*alone in his room, checking his consultants' bills and accounts, using counters*). Three and two make five, plus five ten, and ten more make twenty. Three and two make five. 'In addition, on the twenty-fourth last, one exploratory, preparatory and emollient enema, for the purpose of softening, moistening and refreshing Monsieur Argan's lower bowel'. I like Mr Florid, my apothecary. His bills are phrased so politely. 'M. Argan's lower bowel, thirty sous'. Yes . . . All very well being polite, Mr Florid, but you have to be fair too; you can't go stinging patients like that. Thirty sous for an enema! Got to be some movement there, that'll have to drop down. Otherwise, you know what you can do with it . . . You've only charged twenty sous up till now, and when an apothecary says twenty sous, it's ten he's got in mind. There we are then, ten. 'In addition, on the same date, a strong detergent enema made up of diacatholicon, rhubarb, an edulcorated rose-water infusion, and other preparations as per prescription, for the purpose of cleaning, washing and scrubbing M. Argan's gut, thirty sous'. Ten sous again, if you don't mind. 'In addition, on the evening of the same date, a hepatic, soporific, somniferous julep to help M. Argan sleep, thirty-five sous'. No complaints about that one, it did the trick. Ten, fifteen, sixteen, seventeen and a half sous. 'In addition, on the

twenty-fifth, a tonic purgative made up of fresh cascara and
Levantine senna, as prescribed by Dr Purgeon, to expel
and evacuate M. Argan's bile, four francs'. Ah! Mr Florid,
I'm not taking that lying down! Patients have rights. Dr
Purgeon didn't authorise you to charge four francs. Three
francs it should be. Yes, put three francs down, and I'll
pay . . . half. 'In addition, on the same date, a lenitive and
astringent potion to make M. Argan sleep, thirty sous'. All
right, that's one ten-sous piece, one fifteen-sous. 'In
addition, on the twenty-sixth, a carminative emetic to expel
M. Argan's wind, thirty sous'. Is this a joke? Ten. 'In
addition, M. Argan's enema, repeat dose, same evening.
Thirty sous'. What does he take me for? Ten! 'In addition,
on the twenty-seventh, a double-strength laxative to
invade, break up, and evacuate M. Argan's foul humours,
three francs'. So, that's half, plus one thirty-sous piece.
Now you're talking sense. 'In addition, on the twenty-
eighth, a single dose of skimmed and sweetened whey, to
cleanse, mollify and lenify M. Argan's blood, twenty sous'.
Ten – right away. 'In addition, a fortified cordial made up
of half a gramme of bezoar, with essence of lemon and
pomegranate, as per prescription, five francs'. Steady on,
doctor, that's a touch excessive. If you go on like this,
nobody'll want to be ill any more. Why don't you settle
for half, and I'll add two twenty-sous pieces? Three plus
two, five, another five equals ten, and ten is twenty. Let's
see again: two twenty-sous pieces, six ten-sous, one fifteen-
sous . . . That's sixty-three francs four and a half sous. So
that means this month I must have taken one, two, three,
four, five, six, seven, eight lots of medicine, and one, two,
three, four, five, six, seven, eight, nine, ten, eleven, twelve
enemas. Last month it came to twelve lots of medicine and

twenty enemas. Hmm! Not in the least surprising, that. I haven't been so well this month as last. I'll tell Dr Purgeon, he'll have to get stuck in and do something about it. (*Shouting.*) Somebody come and clear all this away! . . . Nobody there? As usual, I'm wasting good breath. I'm always telling them that I mustn't be left on my own, ever. No use. (*Rings a little bell to summon his servants.*) They don't hear, or don't want to. This damn thing isn't loud enough! Ting-a-ling, ting-a-ling. (*Pause.*) Deafening silence. Ting-a-ling, ting-a-ling. (*Pause.*) There's none so deaf as those who . . . Ting-a-ling, ting-a-ling, where the blazes is everyone? Toinette, ting-a-ling. Just as if I didn't exist. She's a pain in the . . . , she really is! Ting-a-ling. Selfish cow! Ting-a-ling. On top of everything else they want me to burst an artery! (*No longer rings bell, just shouts.*) Ting-a-ling, ting-a-ling, ting-a-ling. She can go to hell, for all I care. Hey, monkey-face, you can't just leave invalids on their own, unattended! Unbelievable. Ting-a-ling, ting-a-ling, ting-a-ling. For crying out loud! Baboon-bum, where are you? Ting-a-ling, ting-a-ling, ting-a-ling. I don't believe this, they *are* going to let me die! Ting-a-ling, ting-a-ling, ting-a-ling!

2. TOINETTE, ARGAN.

TOINETTE (*entering Argan's room*). Here I am!

ARGAN. Ah! You little . . .

TOINETTE (*pretending to have hit her head*). All right, all right . . . Now look what you've made me do, you're so bloody impatient. I was in such a hurry to get here, I hit my head on the corner of a shutter.

ARGAN (*angry*). D'you expect me to believe? . . .

TOINETTE (*to shut him up each time*). Ouch!

ARGAN. I've been waiting . . .

TOINETTE. Ouch!

ARGAN. A whole hour . . .

TOINETTE. Ouch!

ARGAN. And nobody . . .

TOINETTE. Ouch!

ARGAN. Shut up, will you. I'm trying to reduce you to a quivering wreck.

TOINETTE. Oh charming, that's really nice. Just what I need after what I've done to myself.

ARGAN. What about me! I've almost lost my voice, shouting.

TOINETTE. And I've almost lost my head, thanks to you. I call that quits. Agreed?

ARGAN. By God, you *are* a little . . .

TOINETTE. If you go on, I'll cry.

ARGAN. But you just left me for . . .

TOINETTE. Bloody hell!

ARGAN. Foulmouth! . . . Do you want me to? . . .

TOINETTE. Ouch!

ARGAN. Shut up, will you! She won't even give me the pleasure of telling her off!

TOINETTE. Tell me off as much as you like. See if I care.

ARGAN. You won't let me get going. Every time I start, you interrupt.

TOINETTE. Look, if your pleasure's yelling at me, yell. Whatever blows your frock up. But my pleasure's howling, so let me howl.

ARGAN. All right, all right. Truce. Now, get rid of all of this. (*Gets up from his chair.*) Has today's enema taken?

TOINETTE. Taken?

ARGAN. Yes, yes. Did I produce much bile?

TOINETTE. How should I know, for crying out loud? I don't stick my nose into that. That's for your Mr Florid. He's the one that's making the killing.

ARGAN. I've got to take another one in a minute. Go and get some hot water.

TOINETTE. These two . . . medicos, Florid and Purgeon, are having a high old time with you. They're making mincemeat out of you. I'd like to know exactly what sort of illness it is that needs so many medicines.

ARGAN. Don't meddle. This is too hard for you. Fetch my daughter, will you, I want a word with her about a little matter.

TOINETTE. Talk of the devil . . . she must be psychic.

3. ANGÉLIQUE, TOINETTE, ARGAN.

ARGAN. I was just thinking about you, Angélique. Come over here, I want a little word.

ANGÉLIQUE. I'm listening, father.

ARGAN (*hurrying off to toilet*). Just one moment. Pass me my stick. Back in a jiff.

TOINETTE (*mocking*). Hurry, sir, hurry. Goodness, that Mr Florid certainly knows how to get things out of people. The way he worms it out. Talk about time and motion!

4. ANGÉLIQUE, TOINETTE.

ANGÉLIQUE (*lovelorn expression, confiding*). Toinette!

TOINETTE. Yes?

ANGÉLIQUE. Look at me.

TOINETTE. I'm looking.

ANGÉLIQUE. Toinette!

TOINETTE. That's me. Well?

ANGÉLIQUE. Can't you guess?

TOINETTE. Oh, I expect I can. That young man of yours. That's the one subject we keep coming back to. For a whole week now, my dear, you've refused to talk of anything else.

ANGÉLIQUE. I know you think I've got a one-track mind.
Why don't you bring the subject up first, instead of me?

TOINETTE. You never give me the chance. You're straight
in, wham, every time.

ANGÉLIQUE. It's true, I can't stop thinking about him and
talking about him. You do understand, Toinette? I just
can't help it. You're not cross with me?

TOINETTE. Of course I'm not.

ANGÉLIQUE. It can't be wrong to feel the way I do about
him?

TOINETTE. I never said it was.

ANGÉLIQUE. He's got such a way with words!

TOINETTE. Charms birds off trees.

ANGÉLIQUE. Do you think I should make myself deaf to all
the lovely things he says to me?

TOINETTE. Of course I don't.

ANGÉLIQUE. Don't you think it was Destiny that brought
us together? Don't you think we were simply meant for
each other? It just had to be!

TOINETTE. Oh yes.

ANGÉLIQUE. Don't you think it was just so chivalrous the
way he leapt to my defence without even knowing who I
was? What a gentleman!

TOINETTE. Who said the age of romance was dead?

ANGÉLIQUE. Don't you think he's gallant?

TOINETTE. Oh yes.

ANGÉLIQUE. Don't you think he's the most handsome man you've ever seen?

TOINETTE. Oh yes.

ANGÉLIQUE. And so winning?

TOINETTE. Oh yes.

ANGÉLIQUE. And such a gentleman.

TOINETTE. Born and bred.

ANGÉLIQUE. Every word he says is so romantic.

TOINETTE. Oh yes.

ANGÉLIQUE. And isn't it the cruellest thing you ever heard, that we're not allowed to meet and get to know each other properly and show each other our feelings?

TOINETTE. Oh it is.

ANGÉLIQUE. But Toinette, listen, do you think he loves me as much as he says he does?

TOINETTE. Ah, yes, well, these things aren't always what they seem. With some people, real love and make-believe look the same. I've certainly seen some dab-hands in my time.

ANGÉLIQUE. Oh, Toinette, don't say that! He says such lovely things to me, he can't be lying, he can't be!

TOINETTE. You'll find out soon enough. He wrote to you yesterday, didn't he, to tell you he's going to ask permission to marry you? Let's see if he sticks to it. The proof of the pudding . . .

ANGÉLIQUE. Oh, Toinette, if he's lying to me, I'll never believe anything any man says ever again.

TOINETTE. Shh! Your father . . .

5. ARGAN, ANGÉLIQUE, TOINETTE.

ARGAN (*sitting down in his chair*). Well now, Angélique, I'm going to tell you something which I dare say you've not been expecting. I've received an offer of marriage for you. There, what do you think of that? It makes you smile? Lovely word, marriage, isn't it? Definitely a favourite with the girls. Ah, human nature! . . . Anyway, from what I can see, I don't really need to ask if you want to get married.

ANGÉLIQUE. My duty is to obey you always, father.

ARGAN. That's my girl. I've agreed on your behalf, everything's been settled.

ANGÉLIQUE. I must do what you say, father.

ARGAN. Your step-mother thinks I should put you both in a convent, you and your little sister. She's quite adamant it's the best idea.

TOINETTE (*aside*). For her, yes.

ARGAN. She wouldn't agree to this marriage at first. But I've won her round at last, and now it's official.

ANGÉLIQUE. Father, I do want you to know how much I appreciate your kindness.

TOINETTE. Credit where credit's due. I have to hand it to you, this is the most sensible thing I've ever seen you do.

ARGAN. I haven't met the young man yet. But I'm told that we'll be very satisfied with him, both of us.

ANGÉLIQUE. Oh father, I know we will.

ARGAN. How do you know? Have you seen him already?

ANGÉLIQUE. As you've agreed to our marriage, I can tell you . . . everything. We met six days ago, quite by chance. We were instantly attracted towards each other, straightaway. That's why he's asked for my hand.

ARGAN. That's not exactly how it was reported to me, but no matter, if that's what happened, so be it, and everyone can be happy. Apparently he's a good-looking boy, tall.

ANGÉLIQUE. Yes, father.

ARGAN. Good bones, organs. Steady pulse.

ANGÉLIQUE. Undoubtedly.

ARGAN. Pleasant sort of cove.

ANGÉLIQUE. Oh yes.

ARGAN. Strong athletic build.

ANGÉLIQUE. Very athletic.

ARGAN. Steady. Good family background.

ANGÉLIQUE. Couldn't be better.

ARGAN. Reliable.

ANGÉLIQUE. Utterly.

ARGAN. Good command of Latin and Greek.

ANGÉLIQUE. That I couldn't say.

ARGAN. And he's sitting his final medical exams at the moment. He'll be a qualified doctor in a month or so.

ANGÉLIQUE. A doctor?

ARGAN. A doctor, yes. Hasn't he told you?

ANGÉLIQUE. No he hasn't. Who told you?

ARGAN. Dr Purgeon.

ANGÉLIQUE. Does Dr Purgeon know him then?

ARGAN. He ought to, he's his nephew.

ANGÉLIQUE. Cléante, the nephew of Dr Purgeon?

ARGAN. Who's Cléante? We're talking about the young man who wants to marry you.

ANGÉLIQUE. That's what I thought.

ARGAN. The one who wants to marry you is Dr Purgeon's nephew, the son of his brother-in-law, Dr Lillicrap. The lad's name is Thomas, not Cléante. Thomas Lillicrap. We fixed up your marriage this morning, the three of us, Dr Purgeon, Mr Florid and myself. Tomorrow, your fiancé's being brought over by his father to see me. What's the matter? You seem a little surprised.

ANGÉLIQUE. I think we've been talking at cross-purposes. We've been talking about different people.

TOINETTE. It's a farce, sir, this scheme. With all the money you've got, you don't need to marry her off to a doctor.

ARGAN. That's exactly what I'm going to do. You keep out of this, it doesn't concern you.

TOINETTE. Shhh, calm down. Can't we discuss the matter like reasonable, grownup people? For example, perhaps you'd be kind enough to explain to us the reasons behind your decision?

ARGAN. Reasons? You know how I'm suffering. Every illness in the book. I need a doctor for a son-in-law. Even better if he's from a medical family. That way I can have a team of specialists permanently on call. I'll have a whole dispensary available day and night as well . . . absolutely essential if I'm to turn the corner.

TOINETTE. Well, there, that's nice and clear. And logical. You see, nobody had to get steamed up. But, come on now, sir, hand on heart, you're not really ill, are you? Not really, eh?

ARGAN. Not ill? Me? Not ill? How can you . . . ? Of course I'm ill! Don't ever say that again!

TOINETTE. Sorry, sorry. Yes you're ill, no question. Don't let's argue. Very ill, I absolutely agree. Seriously ill. Totally ill. Even iller than you think, if that's possible. A basket of maladies. But your daughter should please herself who she marries. She's not ill, and there's no earthly reason why she should marry a doctor.

ARGAN. It's for my sake that I'm giving her to a doctor. A proper daughter, with proper feelings, would be only too delighted to marry someone who'd be good for her poor father's health.

TOINETTE. I don't know, sir, really I don't. Can I give you a piece of friendly advice?

ARGAN. Depends what it is.

TOINETTE. Put this ridiculous marriage right out of your feverish, addled old noddle.

ARGAN. Why?

TOINETTE. Because your daughter won't do it.

ARGAN. She won't?

TOINETTE. She won't.

ARGAN. Angélique?

TOINETTE. Angélique. She'll tell you that she's got no time for Dr Lillicrap. Or his son Thomas. Or for any other Lillicrap you come up with.

ARGAN. Well, I've got time for this plan because it's going to work out better than you may think. Dr Lillicrap's son is his only heir, and on top of that Dr Purgeon has no children of his own, and intends to leave everything he has to the children of this marriage. Do you know how much he's worth? Eight thousand francs, no less.

TOINETTE. He must have polished off a lot of patients to make that kind of money.

ARGAN. Eight thousand. Not to be sneezed at. And there's the father's estate too. We mustn't forget that.

TOINETTE. That's all well and good, sir, but I come back to my point. I really would advise you to find her another husband. She's just not cut out to be Mrs Lillicrap.

ARGAN. I say she is.

TOINETTE. Don't.

ARGAN. Don't what?

TOINETTE. Say.

ARGAN. Why shouldn't I?

TOINETTE. People will say you've gone off your head.

ARGAN. They can say what they like. I'm telling you, I insist.
   She'll keep the promise I've made.

TOINETTE. She won't.

ARGAN. I'll make her.

TOINETTE. I'm telling you she won't.

ARGAN. I'll put her in a convent.

TOINETTE. You wouldn't.

ARGAN. I would.

TOINETTE. Ha!

ARGAN. What do you mean, ha?

TOINETTE. You'd never put her in a convent.

ARGAN. I'd never put her in a convent?

TOINETTE. You'd never put her in a convent.

ARGAN. Never?

TOINETTE. Never.

ARGAN. Ha ha ha! Very droll. I won't put my own daughter
   in a convent if I want to?

TOINETTE. That's what I said.

ARGAN. Who'll stop me?

TOINETTE. You will.

ARGAN. I will?

TOINETTE. You haven't the heart.

ARGAN. Oh yes I have.

TOINETTE. Who are you kidding?

ARGAN. I'm serious.

TOINETTE. You're too much of a daddy.

ARGAN. I'm not.

TOINETTE. One or two big rolling tears; arms around your
neck; 'daddykins' in your ear; you'll be putty in her hands.

ARGAN. I won't be caught like that.

TOINETTE. You will, you will.

ARGAN. I shan't give an inch.

TOINETTE. You're a fool, sir.

ARGAN. Mind what you're saying!

TOINETTE. I know you. You're a softie, you can't help it.

ARGAN (*getting worked up*). I am not a softie. I can be tough
any time I want. Tough. Tough. Oh yes.

TOINETTE. Easy, sir. Remember you're not well.

ARGAN. She'll marry the man I say she'll marry. That's
final. She'd better start getting used to it.

TOINETTE. She won't. You'd better start getting used to that.

ARGAN. What's the world coming to? Staff speaking to quality like that!

TOINETTE. When the quality doesn't see the cock-up he's making, he's got to be sorted out.

ARGAN (*running after* TOINETTE). You cheeky little . . . ! Now you've gone too far!

TOINETTE (*fleeing*). You pay me to stop you doing things you'll only be sorry for.

ARGAN (*angrily chasing her around his chair, waving his stick*). Come here! Wait! I'll teach you to talk like that!

TOINETTE (*fleeing, and dodging around Argan's chair*). I only want to make you see sense.

ARGAN. Meddler!

TOINETTE. I'll never give my consent to this marriage.

ARGAN. Pig-head!

TOINETTE. I won't have her marrying Thomas Lillicrap.

ARGAN. Feminist!

TOINETTE. She'll do what I say, not you.

ARGAN. Angélique, help me, will you. Stop her.

ANGÉLIQUE. Calm down, daddy, you'll only make yourself ill.

ARGAN. If you don't stop her wicked schemes, Angélique, I'll have nothing further to do with you.

TOINETTE. And if she obeys you, I'll cut her off without a penny.

ARGAN (*slumps into his chair, exhausted by the chase*). Ouf! Ouf!
I can't go on. This'll be the death of me.

6. BÉLINE, ANGÉLIQUE, TOINETTE, ARGAN.

ARGAN. Ah, here's my wife! Come here, come here.

BÉLINE. What's the matter, you poor thing?

ARGAN. You've saved my life.

BÉLINE. What's been happening, petal?

ARGAN. Sweetie.

BÉLINE. Babykins.

ARGAN. They've been getting me all upset.

BÉLINE. There, there! Poor darling. Tell mummy all about it.

ARGAN. That nasty horrid Toinette's getting cheekier than
ever.

BÉLINE. Don't get upset.

ARGAN. She makes me so angry.

BÉLINE. Shhh! Sweetums.

ARGAN. She's been arguing with everything I say. For a
whole hour!

BÉLINE. Try and calm down.

ARGAN. She had the nerve to say I'm not ill.

BÉLINE. What a cheek.

ARGAN. You know how bad I am, don't you, dearest?

BÉLINE. Yes, yes, she was very naughty.

ARGAN. She'll drive me to an early grave.

BÉLINE. Shhh.

ARGAN. She's the cause of all these bilious attacks.

BÉLINE. Don't get upset.

ARGAN. I've been asking you for heaven knows how long to get rid of her.

BÉLINE. But, poppet, the servant without some sort of shortcoming hasn't been invented. Some are bad, and others are not so bad, and you have to put up with it. Toinette's good at her work, she's careful and conscientious, and above all she's not on the fiddle. Servants like that you don't grow on trees . . . Toinette!

TOINETTE. Madame.

BÉLINE. Why have you been upsetting my husband?

TOINETTE (*sugary*). Me, madame? I'm sure I don't know what you mean. I try to serve Monsieur Argan in every possible way.

ARGAN. Little liar!

TOINETTE. He told us he wanted to marry his daughter to Dr Lillicrap's son. I said it would be a very good catch for her, but that he still ought to put her in a convent.

BÉLINE. I see nothing wrong in that. Toinette's right.

ARGAN. You don't really mean that. She's wicked, and she's behaved atrociously to me.

BÉLINE. All right, darling, I believe you. There, crisis over. It's not a drama. Toinette, you must understand that if you upset my husband again, I shall dismiss you. Give me his dressing gown and some pillows. I'll settle him into his chair. You don't look at all comfortable. Pull your night-cap down. The surest way to catch cold is through the ears.

ARGAN. My angel. How can I ever show you how grateful I am? All your care and attention.

BÉLINE (*arranging Argan's pillows*). Sit up a moment, so I can put these under you. This one to lean on here, and this one on here. Lie back on this one, and we'll pop the last one under your head.

TOINETTE (*putting a pillow firmly down on his head, then running off*). And this one to keep the mildew away.

ARGAN (*getting up and throwing all the pillows at Toinette*). So now you're a murderer?

BÉLINE. What's the matter?

ARGAN (*out of breath; falls into his chair*). I can't stand it!

BÉLINE. Why do you get so worked up? She was only trying to help.

ARGAN. You don't understand how tricky she is, my love. Now I'm in a state again. I'll need at least eight prescriptions and twelve enemas to sort this out.

BÉLINE. There, there, my little lamb, don't fret so.

ARGAN. Oh Béline, you're my only consolation.

BÉLINE. Poor little martyr!

ARGAN. Listen, pussikin, I want to do one big, special thing, a monument of my love for you. I've mentioned it before, I'm going to make my will.

BÉLINE. Oh no, oh dear no, let's have none of that. I don't want to hear that kind of talk, I don't even want to think about it. The mere mention of wills makes me shudder.

ARGAN. I did ask you to have a word with our notary, didn't I?

BÉLINE. He's here. I brought him along with me.

ARGAN. Show him in. What are we waiting for? (*Pause.*) Well?

BÉLINE. I'm sorry, my darling. It's just that when one loves one's husband as much as I do, one doesn't think straight.

7. MR GOODFELLOW, BÉLINE, ARGAN.

ARGAN. Come in, Mr Goodfellow, come in. Have a seat. My wife has told me all about you. I'd like both of your opinions on the will I propose to make.

BÉLINE. Oh no, please! Leave me out of this, I don't understand any of it.

MR GOODFELLOW. Your good wife has explained your intentions to me, what it is you have in mind for her. I have to tell you that you can't leave her anything in your will.

ARGAN. Why not?

MR GOODFELLOW. It's prohibited here in Paris under an ancient law. It would be another matter, of course, in those legislative areas where the new family law operates. But here, your will would be null and void. The only provision a man and wife can make for each other is by mutual gift during the lifetime of both. On top of that, there must be no children, whether by that marriage or any previous one contracted by either party, at the time of the decease of the testatur.

ARGAN. What kind of law is that, not allowing a husband to leave anything to a wife who's been loving and devoted? I'll look for a lawyer, a barrister, anyone, and find a way out of this.

MR GOODFELLOW. I wouldn't recommend it. They're usually extremely strict about this kind of thing, they're concerned with the letter of the law, not the spirit. They see things in black and white, there's nothing grey about it. There are other people you could speak to who are more amenable, who know all about the grey areas. They don't actually break any law, they're just broad-minded about the rules. You see what I'm trying to say. Ah well, where would we be without them? Live and let live. If there was no leeway in this profession one would simply starve.

ARGAN. My wife told me what a clever man you are, very above board. Tell me what I should do, then, to make sure she inherits all my estate. My children mustn't get their hands on it.

MR GOODFELLOW. What do you do? You choose a

reliable friend of your wife, say nothing about it, and put all you can in trust to him or her. Then, at an appropriate date, that friend transfers it to your wife. Conversely, you could contract a large number of obligations to various creditors. They'd allow their names to be used on your wife's behalf, at the same time giving her a written guarantee that they're legally making her a gift. Or, thirdly, you could simply give her cash instalments, using different accounts. It's quite simple.

BÉLINE. Don't go on! If anything happened to this little mite, I wouldn't want to go on living. Really, I wouldn't, my love.

ARGAN. My treasure!

BÉLINE. My world would fall apart if I lost you.

ARGAN. What a wonderful wife you are!

BÉLINE. Life wouldn't be worth that to me!

ARGAN. Angel!

BÉLINE. I'd follow you to the grave just to prove how much I loved you!

ARGAN. Dear darling, you'll break my heart. Don't get so upset, please don't.

MR GOODFELLOW. Tears aren't necessary, we haven't reached that stage yet.

BÉLINE. Oh, Mr Goodfellow, you don't know what it is to love a husband as I love mine.

ARGAN. If I die, the only regret I'll have, my love, is that you and I never had a child. Dr Purgeon did promise me that he'd make sure I could do it.

MR GOODFELLOW. I'm sure you can rise to the occasion.

ARGAN. I must make out my will, precious, the way Mr Goodfellow recommends. But as a precaution I'm going to give you twenty thousand francs in gold. They're under the floorboards in my study. I'll give you a couple of bonds as well, which you can cash in whenever you choose.

BÉLINE. I don't want it . . . How much did you say was under the floorboards?

ARGAN. Twenty thousand francs, my dumpling.

BÉLINE. I won't hear any more talk of money . . . How much are the bonds worth?

ARGAN. Four thousand francs one, six thousand the other, sweetheart.

BÉLINE. Money! You can be swimming in the stuff for all I care, but if you haven't got love, you're the poorest person in the world.

ARGAN. That came straight from the heart, my precious.

MR GOODFELLOW. Shall we get on with the will?

ARGAN. We'd be more comfortable in my study. Your arm, my love.

BÉLINE. Come along, cabbage.

8. ANGÉLIQUE, TOINETTE.

TOINETTE. They're in there with the notary. I heard them mention the word 'will'. Your step-mother doesn't miss a trick. I bet that at this precise moment she's separating you and Louison from your inheritance.

[handwritten margin note: Wise voice of play]

ANGÉLIQUE. He can do what he likes with his money, I really don't care. Just so long as he doesn't tell me who to marry . . . But that's exactly what he *is* doing, Toinette. It's dreadful. Help me, please, tell me what to do. I can't bear it. *[handwritten: relies on T.]*

TOINETTE. I'll help you, silly thing, you know you can always rely on me. To be perfectly honest, I've never had any time for your step-mother, always trying to get round me. Well, it doesn't wash, I'm on your side. I'll have to change tactics, though, if I'm to help you. I'll pretend I don't care what happens to you. I'll go along with the plot your father and step-mother are hatching.

ANGÉLIQUE. And please find some way to tell Cléante what's happening.

TOINETTE. I could get my . . . friend, the one I call Mr Punchinello, to take a message. I'll have to whisper some sweet nothings in his ear, but, ah well, for you . . . It's a bit late today, but first thing tomorrow I'll find him and I'm sure he'll be delighted.

BÉLINE. Toinette!

TOINETTE. Her Ladyship calls. Bye. Count on me.

First Interlude

Change to street scene. PUNCHINELLO *enters, to serenade his lady under cover of dark. He is interrupted first by violins, making him angry; then by the night-watch, made up of dancers and musicians.*

PUNCHINELLO. Oh, love, love, love! Punchinello, have you gone raving mad? What's your game? What are you playing at? You never do a day's work these days, your business is going down the plug. You can't eat, can't drink, can't sleep, and for what? For a dragon, a tyrant who walks all over you, whatever you do or say. Oh, no self-pity. I'm caught in the tender trap. Love's a madness, a disease. Not exactly ideal for a man of my age, but there you go! You can't be sensible at the snap of a finger. A pensioner can fall head over heels as much as a teenager. I've come to try to tame my jungle-cat with a serenade. Sometimes a lump-in-the-throat lament outside her door can melt a sweet lover. I'll strum along on this. (*Picks up an instrument*) Night, o gentle night, slide my song of love up under her bedclothes! (*Sings*)

Night and day, you are the one,
Oh please say yes, or I'm undone!
But say no and I'll go.
I'll moan at the moon
And howl at the sun.

I live in hope,
I watch the clock.

It's such a shock:
How can I cope?

I dream that I'm crooning
Your name to the stars.
I'm in my bed swooning,
But I'm still behind bars
In your prison of love!

Night and day, you are the one,
Oh please say yes, or I'm undone!
But say no and I'll go.
I'll moan at the moon
And howl at the sun.

If you can't sleep,
Come and have a peep
At the all-over bruise
You've made of me,
My loving, tender Muse!

Say you've been wrong
To use me so.
One word and I'll go.

Night and day, you are the one,
Oh please say yes, or I'm undone!
But say no and I'll go.
I'll moan at the moon
And howl at the sun.

An old woman appears at the window and makes fun of
PUNCHINELLO *as she sings:*

OLD WOMAN: Ah! You young men, you're all the same,
Faithful for just one day!

For you it's one big game,
Then pack bags and creep away.
Trust men?
I won't again.
It's the morals of the pig-sty.
A girl should have a good think why
She'd believe a single word you said.
Better dead than bed
With a sack of testosterone.
Want some advice, girls?
Keep yourself to yourself, it's more fun on your own.

Dance and music. Orchestra punctuates the next speech.

PUNCHINELLO. What was that cacophony? Violins, shhh!
Let me have a nice and private moan about my gut-
wrenching love. Knock it off, will you? Shut it! Did you
hear me? Oi! Is this some kind of a joke? You'll bust my
ear-drums. Hey! I'll get upset. And I'm not a pretty sight
when I get upset . . . Thank God! . . . What, again? Bloody
violins! Put out the cat! (PUNCHINELLO *sings to drown out
violins.*) La, la la la, la. (*Pretending to play an instrument.*) Plink,
plank, plonk. Well, this is fun. I'll show you, scrapers and
pluckers. This'll shut you up. Musicians are bastards.
Right, now, before my piece of resistance, I must tune up
properly. Plink, plank, plonk. No, wind's in the wrong
direction. Plink, plank, plonk. The weather's got at the
strings. Plink, plank, plonk . . . Someone's coming. Just let
me put this down . . .

CONSTABLES (*coming down the street, singing*). Who goes there?
Who goes there?

PUNCHINELLO. Who the hell is this, now? Am I in some
sort of opera?

CONSTABLES. Who goes there? Who goes there? Who goes there?

PUNCHINELLO (*alarmed*). It's me! It's me!

CONSTABLES. Who's me, exactly?

PUNCHINELLO. Just me. I told you: me.

CONSTABLES. And who are *you*?

PUNCHINELLO. Me, me, me, me, me, me!

CONSTABLES. Name, rank, number! Jump to it!

PUNCHINELLO (*swaggering*). My name's . . . Count . . . Yerblessings.

CONSTABLES. Over here, lads! That joker's over here.

Dance. The night-watch hunt for PUNCHINELLO. *Next speech is punctuated by music and dance.*

PUNCHINELLO. Who goes there? Hark, do I hear fairies? This way, my people. I'm coming to get you now. Save yourselves while you can! I'll cut you to ribbons! Messrs Champagne, Poitevin, Picard, Basque and Breton! Pass me my musket. (*Pretends to fire it.*) Bang! (*They all fall, get up and flee.*) Ha ha ha! That showed 'em. I'm scared of them; they're petrified of me! If you're going to tell porkies, make 'em big and juicy. What saved my bacon? Putting on the lardy-da.

Constables move in close, hear what he says, and grab him.

CONSTABLES. Got him! Give us a hand here, lads.

Dance. The whole night-watch approach, carrying lanterns.

CONSTABLES. You bastard, tried to frighten us? You dog-breath, snot-rag, turd-sack, bog-pile, piss-pant – frighten us!

PUNCHINELLO. Gentlemen, I was plastered.

CONSTABLES. Plastered, did you hear him, boys? Well now, we're going to do the plastering. You wait. In jug for starters.

PUNCHINELLO. I've done nothing.

CONSTABLES. Clink.

PUNCHINELLO. What *have* I done?

CONSTABLES. Cooler.

PUNCHINELLO. Let go, if you'd be so good.

CONSTABLES. No.

PUNCHINELLO. Please.

CONSTABLES. No.

PUNCHINELLO. Go on.

CONSTABLES. No.

PUNCHINELLO. Just move your arms.

CONSTABLES. No.

PUNCHINELLO. A fraction.

CONSTABLES. No.

PUNCHINELLO. If I ask you nicely?

CONSTABLES. No.

PUNCHINELLO. If I smile sweetly?

CONSTABLES. No.

PUNCHINELLO. You wouldn't hurt an old man?

CONSTABLES. Stuff it! Not another word!
    We'll teach you. You heard.
    You're doing bird.

PUNCHINELLO. Gentlemen, is there no arrangement you
    can think of . . . to oil this particular lock?

CONSTABLES. Well, we're not hard men. In fact,
    A softer touch would be hard to find.
    A handful of banknotes might swing it.

PUNCHINELLO. Search me, gentlemen, no wallet.

CONSTABLES. Oh dear, oh dear!
    The choice is clear.
    It's pinchin' and pokin',
    Or every bone broken.

PUNCHINELLO. Let's see . . . Erm, yes. Pinchin' and pokin'.

CONSTABLES. Brace yourself.

Dance. The constables push him about, pinch him etc. to the music.

PUNCHINELLO. One, two, three, four, five, six, seven,
    eight, nine, ten, eleven, twelve, and thirteen and fourteen
    makes fifteen.

CONSTABLES. I think we missed one. Start again.

PUNCHINELLO. Ooh ooh! My head! It's splitting. Do my
    bones instead. I'll go for broke . . .

    Just a joke.

CONSTABLES. Fair enough, whatever you say.

Dance. The constables beat him in rhythm.

PUNCHINELLO. All right, all right. Oh look, I've found my wallet!

CONSTABLES. Now there's a decent bloke.
And he does like a joke.

PUNCHINELLO. Gentlemen, goodnight.

CONSTABLES. Ta ta.

PUNCHINELLO. Au reservoir.

CONSTABLES. Toodloo.

PUNCHINELLO. Till we meet again.

CONSTABLES. Don't know where, don't know when.
But why not, some rainy day?

Act Two

1. TOINETTE, CLÉANTE.

TOINETTE. What is it you want, sir?

CLÉANTE. Who? Want? Me?

TOINETTE. Oh, it's you. What are you doing here?

CLÉANTE. Discovering my fate. And I want to talk to my
darling Angélique. Those mad marriage plans I've been
hearing about. I must know how she feels.

TOINETTE. All right. But don't go charging in, all guns
blazing, not with Angélique. You've got to be subtle, play
it, play it . . . You know they're watching her like hawks,
for a start? She's not allowed out, nobody can talk to her
and she can talk to nobody. In fact, it's only because her
auntie's got a soft spot for her that we were able to go to
the theatre that evening, when you two first set eyes on
each other. And we've made very sure not to mention that.

CLÉANTE. And that's precisely why I'm not here now as
Cléante, the man in love with her, but as a friend of her
music teacher. He's said I can stand in for him.

TOINETTE. Here comes her father. Go over there, by the
door, and I'll announce you.

2. ARGAN, TOINETTE, CLÉANTE.

ARGAN. Dr Purgeon told me to stride up and down my
room every morning, twelve times. But I forgot to ask if he
meant lengths or widths.

TOINETTE. Sir, there's a . . .

ARGAN. Not so loud! Stupid woman, you'll split my head
open. Don't you know that the sick must always be
addressed in a whisper?

TOINETTE. I wanted to tell you . . .

ARGAN. I told you, in a whisper.

TOINETTE. Sir . . . (*She pretends to speak; no sound.*)

ARGAN. What?

TOINETTE. I said . . . (*Pretending to speak; no sound.*)

ARGAN. What are you saying?

TOINETTE (*aloud*). I said there's someone here who wants to
speak to you.

ARGAN. Show him in.

TOINETTE *gestures* CLÉANTE *to come closer.*

CLÉANTE. Sir . . .

TOINETTE (*mocking*). Shhh, not so loud. You'll split his head.

CLÉANTE. Sir, I'm delighted to see that you're up and about
and obviously so much better.

TOINETTE (*pretending to be angry*). What do you mean, better?
What rubbish! Sir? Sir's always ill.

CLÉANTE. Someone said his honour was in better health, and if looks are anything to go by, he certainly looks well.

TOINETTE. What d'you mean, 'looks well'? He looks awful, and anyone who says anything else is a troublemaker. His honour's never been as bad as this.

ARGAN. She's right.

TOINETTE. He may eat, drink, walk and sleep like anyone else. But don't be fooled, he's ill.

ARGAN. That's a fact.

CLÉANTE. I'm terribly sorry. I'm here on behalf of your daughter's music teacher. He's had to leave town for a day or two, and I'm here in his place. I'm a very dear friend. He's concerned that there shouldn't be any gaps in your daughter's lessons, in case she forgets what she's already learnt.

ARGAN. Good, good. Fetch Angélique.

TOINETTE. Don't you think, sir, it would be a better idea to take this gentleman to her room instead?

ARGAN. No, no, bring her here.

TOINETTE. He can't give her proper lessons unless they're alone.

ARGAN. Oh yes he can.

TOINETTE. Your head will only start spinning, and you know you mustn't have any excitement in your present state. We mustn't bludgeon your poor old brains.

ARGAN. You heard what I said. I like music, and I'd find it

very . . . Ah! here she comes. Toinette, go and see if my wife's got dressed yet.

3. ARGAN, ANGÉLIQUE, CLÉANTE.

ARGAN. Come here, child. Your music teacher has gone off somewhere out of town. This is his replacement. He'll give you your lesson.

ANGÉLIQUE. Oh my God!

ARGAN. What's the matter?

ANGÉLIQUE. It's . . .

ARGAN. It's what?

ANGÉLIQUE. It's . . . very odd.

ARGAN. Go on.

ANGÉLIQUE. Last night, I dreamt I was in the most awful situation, and that someone who was the spitting image of this gentleman appeared. I asked him to help me, and he sorted everything out. So you can see what an amazing coincidence it is . . . the person who filled my thoughts all night long . . . in this very room.

CLÉANTE. Awake or asleep, I'm delighted to fill Mademoiselle's thoughts. My happiness would be total if she asked me to sort out all her problems. Ask anything you like, I'd –

4. TOINETTE, CLÉANTE, ANGÉLIQUE, ARGAN.

TOINETTE (*mocking*). Sir, I must swallow my words and go
back on what I was saying yesterday. I'm now entirely on
your side. Messrs Lillicrap father and son have just arrived.
You won't be so much losing a daughter as gaining a . . .
You're about to see before you the most gorgeous, the
wittiest young man you've ever clapped eyes on. He only
had to speak half a sentence and I was mesmerised! What a
specimen! I almost fainted. Your daughter won't know
what hit her.

ARGAN (*to* CLÉANTE, *who is on the point of leaving*). Please
don't go. I've decided that my daughter should get
married, and the person we're talking about is her fiancé.
She hasn't met him yet.

CLÉANTE. You're doing me too great an honour, asking me
to be present at such a joyful first encounter.

ARGAN. He's the son of a magnificent doctor. The wedding's
in four days.

CLÉANTE. So happy for you.

ARGAN. Do tell her music teacher. He must come.

CLÉANTE. I shall.

ARGAN. And you're invited as well.

CLÉANTE. How kind.

TOINETTE. Come on, everyone in their places. They're
here.   acting.

5. DR LILLICRAP, THOMAS, ARGAN, ANGÉLIQUE, CLÉANTE, TOINETTE.

ARGAN (*putting his hand on his nightcap without taking it off*). Dr Purgeon has strictly forbidden me to uncover my head, gentlemen. Dr Lillicrap, what would happen if I did?

DR LILLICRAP. Professionally or socially, all our visits are designed to help the sick, not to inconvenience them.

ARGAN. It's a great pleasure for me . . .

DR LILLICRAP. We're here today . . .

ARGAN. To welcome you today . . .

DR LILLICRAP. My son Thomas and I . . .

ARGAN. The honour you're doing us . . .

DR LILLICRAP. To show you, sir . . .

ARGAN. I would have wished . . .

DR LILLICRAP. The great pleasure it gives us both . . .

ARGAN. I'd have paid you a visit . . .

DR LILLICRAP. That you have graciously consented . . .

ARGAN. To assure you of the strength . . .

DR LILLICRAP. To welcome us here . . .

ARGAN. But you know . . .

DR LILLICRAP. To honour . . .

ARGAN. That being so sick . . .

DR LILLICRAP. The union of our . . .

ARGAN. I've no choice but . . .

DR LILLICRAP. Let me assure you . . .

ARGAN. To tell you here . . .

DR LILLICRAP. That in all medical matters which may arise . . .

ARGAN. That I'll miss no opportunity . . .

DR LILLICRAP. And indeed in any other . . .

ARGAN. To let you know . . .

DR LILLICRAP. We'll always be, sir . . .

ARGAN. That I'm entirely at your service . . .

DR LILLICRAP. At your service. (*Turns to his son.*) Thomas, walk this way. Introduce yourself properly. Say your piece.

THOMAS (*a gawky oaf straight out of school; gauche and clumsy*). I start with the father, don't I?

DR LILLICRAP. That's right.

THOMAS. Sir, I am here to salute, to recognise, cherish and revere a second father. That second father is you, to whom I would go as far as saying that I owe an even greater debt than to the first. The first gave me corporeal existence, but you have chosen me. He took me out of ineluctable necessity, you accepted me out of nothing less than pure grace. I am the fruit of his loins; but you have exercised your will when you chose to create me. And, in the very way that the spiritual faculties are superior to those of the body, so I owe you the greater debt, and esteem all the more precious this future filiation, for the creation of which

I have come today to offer in advance my profound, my humble gratitude.

TOINETTE. Long live higher education! *down to earth*

THOMAS. All right, father?

DR LILLICRAP. Optime.

ARGAN (*to* ANGÉLIQUE). Don't just stand there. Curtsey.

THOMAS. Do I kiss her now?

DR LILLICRAP. Yes, yes.

THOMAS (*to* ANGÉLIQUE). Madame, it is with its unerring justice that Providence has bestowed upon you the name of mother-in-law, since one . . .

ARGAN. That's not my wife, it's my daughter.

THOMAS. Where's the wife?

ARGAN. She'll be here.

THOMAS. Father, should I wait till she gets here?

DR LILLICRAP. Get on with the speech to the young lady.

THOMAS. Mademoiselle, even as the statue of Memnon issued forth a harmonious note whenever the sun's shafts bathed it in light, so in a like manner do I feel myself brought to life by a gentle rapture in the presence of your golden, radiant charms. And, just as naturalists have observed that the heliotrope, the aptly named sunflower, ceaselessly turns towards the star of day, so my heart from this day forward shall always turn towards the two splendid heavenly bodies which are your eyes, as if towards the magnetic pole insistently drawing to itself that organ, my heart. Permit me, mademoiselle, to lay on the altar of your beauty the gift of this, my heart, which beats with no other ambition than to be, mademoiselle, your very humble, very obedient servant, wedded henceforth and until death us do part, to you.

TOINETTE (*mocking*). What a way with words! Scholar and poet, rolled into one!

ARGAN. Hey, you, what d'you say to that?

CLÉANTE. The gentleman is a linguistic sorcerer, and if he's as fine a doctor as he is an orator, it'll be a remarkable experience to be one of his patients.

TOINETTE. If he writes prescriptions the way he talks . . .

ARGAN. Now then, get me my chair, quick. Everyone sit down. You there, Angélique. Dr Lillicrap, you can see how your boy's impressed us. All I can say is, you're lucky indeed to have a lad like him.

DR LILLICRAP. My dear sir, it's not because I happen to be his father that I can say I'm well pleased with him. Everyone finds him quite . . . transparent. He's never been burdened with what you might call an over-lively imagination. He's not as quick-witted as some folk. But that's precisely what gives me faith in his sound good sense – a quality essential, after all, in our profession. Even when he was still a little boy, he wasn't silly and impertinent. No, no, no. He was docile, gentle. Kept his own counsel. Never went in for what people call 'children's games'. He was . . . unhurried in learning to read, and in fact he was nine before he mastered his ABC. 'Never mind', I said to myself, 'late flowering trees bring forth the best fruit. It's harder to write on marble than on sand; but what's written on marble lasts, while insubstantial sand soon vanishes. This drip-feed way of learning, this caution of the imagination surely mark a subtle and certain mind in the making'. When I sent him to medical school, he struggled a little. But he soon got the bit between his teeth, and his teachers made a point of praising his industry and application. Anyway, by dint of sheer perseverance he passed his exams, and I can tell you in all objectivity that for the final two years of his studies there has been no candidate more in the thick of the intellectual fray than Thomas. He's become a formidable debater, fearsome in his passion to argue against any proposition at all. His arguments are watertight, he's a lion in his defence of principles, he won't be shaken from his opinions, he pursues his dialectical reasoning with punishing, ruthless logic. But what pleases me most of all – and this is where you can see that he's the true son of his father – is that he has an absolute and blind faith in the old school of *plays up* medicine. He won't have any truck with those so-called *to Argan* new discoveries, all that rubbish about blood circulating, and other 'scientific facts' of the same kidney.

THOMAS (*taking a large rolled-up thesis which he presents to* ANGÉLIQUE). I've had this thesis accepted. It attacks the charlatans of the circulation school. With your permission, sir, I'd like to present it to mademoiselle. In the burgeoning harvest of my intellect, this is the first crop.

ANGÉLIQUE. It's of no use to me, sir. I wouldn't understand a thing.

TOINETTE. Oh, give it to me. Yes, crop's the word. Nice

drawings too. Shall we paper the bedroom wall with this crop, with this . . . thesis?

THOMAS. Again with your permission, sir, may I invite mademoiselle one day soon to the hospital to see a woman being dissected? I could explain the various stages of the process.

TOINETTE. Enchanting. Captivating. Some men take the women in their life to theatres of another sort. But to see a body sliced up, well, that's so much more seductive. I mean, what woman wouldn't swoon?

DR LILLICRAP. Let me add that as far as the prerequisites for marriage and the propagation of the species are concerned, you may rest assured that he's exactly as anyone would desire. I've been through our medical checklist. In the reproduction department, he's entirely equipped. The balances, levels and counts to make healthy babies are spot on.

ARGAN. Isn't it your intention, sir, to launch him at court and to establish him as a doctor there?

DR LILLICRAP. To be absolutely frank with you, it's never seemed desirable to me to practise our craft among the great and the famous. I've always felt that we were much better employed serving the general public. They're so much more accommodating. You don't have to answer to anybody for anything you do, and so long as you go by the book, there's no need to worry about any comeback. What's so irritating about upper-class patients is that whenever they fall ill, they insist that their doctors get them well again.

can them off! ironic

A doesn't want to get better

TOINETTE. That really takes the biscuit! Who do they think they are, demanding that you actually cure them? No, your job is to write prescriptions and collect your fees; theirs is to get better if they can. That's the proper division of labour.

DR LILLICRAP. Our one obligation is to follow the code of practice.

ARGAN (*to* CLÉANTE). Now sir, why don't you get my daughter to sing to us?

CLÉANTE. Delighted. I thought it might amuse you all if I were to join the young lady in a duet from the latest cantata. (*To* ANGÉLIQUE, *giving her a sheet of paper.*) This is your part.

ANGÉLIQUE. For me?

CLÉANTE (*aside*). Don't ask questions. Just go along with it, and I'll explain what we're going to sing. Read between the lines. (*Aloud.*) You must bear with me, I'm not the world's greatest singer. The main thing is to listen to mademoiselle.

ARGAN. I hope it tells a nice story.

CLÉANTE. It's a kind of improvised operetta in what you might call rhythmic prose, free verse, something like that. The kind of spontaneous language you'd expect of two people who have to use every subterfuge to get across how they feel about each other.

ARGAN. Subterfuge? Good. We're listening.

CLÉANTE (*using the name of a shepherd, he tells his love how he fell in love with her at first sight, and then in song they tell each other their feelings*). This is the subject of the interlude. A young shepherd is watching the opening scene of a theatrical

shepherd is watching the opening scene of a theatrical
entertainment. He is distracted by a disturbance nearby.
He turns round and sees some lout insulting a young
woman. Instantly he goes to the rescue of what men like to
call the weaker sex. He sees off this lout. Then he turns to
look at the girl. What he sees is a young thing with the
most beautiful eyes imaginable, shedding the most
wonderful tears in the world! He is outraged by the abuse
aimed at such a creature, moved by her tears, beautiful,
beautiful tears. He wants to dry them for her. The young
lady thanks him for his timely intervention, but in such a
charming, such a warm way, with such feeling, that the
young shepherd positively melts. Her every glance, her
every word, burns into his soul. 'Did I', he asks, 'did I
really do anything to deserve such sweet thanks? Any man
would be only too enchanted, run any risk, go to any
lengths, to earn such a display of gratitude'. The whole of
the performance he has come to see goes by unnoticed. Its
only drawback is that it doesn't last long enough. From
that first encounter, from that very first moment, he is in
the grip of a wild love, as if it had already existed for years
and years. He wanders round in a daze. Without her,
without this one being, the world is empty, nobody exists.
He does all he can to find her but is thwarted at every turn.
The young lady is kept well away from prying eyes. But his
need is so urgent that he manages to get a note to her. He
has written her a marriage proposal. She accepts. But at
the same time he hears that her father has arranged for her
to marry someone else. Apparently everything is in place
for the wedding ceremony. You can imagine how the
shepherd feels! The pain, the desolation! Desperate with
jealousy, he devises a scheme to get himself invited into her

house. He must find out what she herself thinks, what the future holds for him. His worst fears are confirmed. The wedding preparations have been made. He witnesses his rival's entrance, <u>a preposterous young man who owes his good luck entirely to the capriciousness of her father</u>. To see such a travesty of justice, to see the natural order stood on its head, makes him so angry that he almost explodes. He darts looks of anguish at the girl, but out of respect for her and because her father is there, that's absolutely all he can do. In the end, he throws caution to the wind, and bursting with love, sings these words to her:

Singing.

'Fair Phyllis, this silence is killing me,
Speak, say something, say what you think of me,
Tell me my destiny!
What will become of me?'

ANGÉLIQUE (*also singing*).
'Look how I am, Tircis – disconsolate.
This nightmare marriage I must consummate.
Yet I only have eyes for you.
I sigh, I cry, I look to the sky.
If I have to go through with it, I'll die.'

ARGAN. Well, well, well, who'd have thought my daughter could sight-read so easily!

CLÉANTE. 'Alas! Fairest Phyllis,
How could love-sick Tircis
Know that for him
There was room
In your bosom?'

ANGÉLIQUE. 'Indeed there's room, more than ever before.
    Oh Tircis, Tircis, it's you I adore!'

CLÉANTE. 'Oh words so full of delight!
    Dearest Phyllis, did I hear you right?
    Say it again, just to make double sure.'

ANGÉLIQUE. 'Yes, Tircis, it's you I adore.
    I love you.'

CLÉANTE. 'Oh God! Again!'

ANGÉLIQUE. 'I love you.'

CLÉANTE. 'Again and again and again. Don't stop.'

ANGÉLIQUE. 'I love you, I love you, I love you.
    Dear Tircis, have I told you I love you?'

CLÉANTE. 'Kings, lords, princes, gods, up there on your
        thrones,
    You've never tasted happiness like my own!
    But sweetest Phyllis, there's a vile infection
    Which will plunge me into black dejection.
    That other man, that rival . . . '

ANGÉLIQUE. 'Ah! I loathe him! Everything about him's
        evil.
    A plague-ridden rat that's crawled up a drain!
    His very existence causes me pain.
    Let's deal with this rat . . . Do I make myself plain?'

CLÉANTE. 'Plain, my belovèd, yet never so fair.
    But when I hear your father declare . . . '

ANGÉLIQUE. 'Let him declare!
    I'd rather die

Than comply,
Much rather die, much rather, rather,
Much rather die, die, die, my father,
Than . . . '

ARGAN. And what does the father have to say in all this?

CLÉANTE. Nothing.

ARGAN. What kind of father is that? What a fool, to put up with this nonsense without saying a word!

CLÉANTE. 'Ah! My belovèd, my . . . '

ARGAN. Yes, quite, we heard you the first time. This little play sets a very bad example. The shepherd Tircis is impertinent, and that Phyllis lacks heart, she shows none of the normal care and consideration due to a father. Show me that bit of paper. Aha, now where exactly do I find the words you were singing? All I can see here are musical notes.

CLÉANTE. But surely you know, sir, that a new system of writing words into the music has just been invented.

ARGAN. If you say so, I must believe you. I bid you good day, and I must say we could have done without your impertinent little cantata.

CLÉANTE. I was only trying to please.

ARGAN. Stupidity is never pleasing. Ah, here's my wife.

6. BÉLINE, ARGAN, TOINETTE, ANGÉLIQUE,
   DR LILLICRAP, THOMAS.

ARGAN. My love, let me introduce Dr Lillicrap's son.

THOMAS (*begins a compliment he has learnt, but his memory fails him, and he cannot finish it.*) Madame, it is with unerring justice that Providence has bestowed upon you the name of mother-in-law, since one beholds on your face . . .

BÉLINE. Young man, I'm happy to have arrived in time to give myself the pleasure of meeting you.

THOMAS. . . . since one beholds on your face . . . since one beholds on your face . . . Madame, you've broken into my flow. I've lost my place.

DR LILLICRAP. Thomas, save it for another occasion.

ARGAN. I wish you'd been here earlier, dear.

TOINETTE. Oh yes, madame, you missed out on the 'second father', and the 'statue of Memnon', and the 'flower called the heliotrope'.

ARGAN. Now then, Angélique, you and the young gentleman should join hands and make a promise.

ANGÉLIQUE. Oh father!

ARGAN. Now why that tone of voice?

ANGÉLIQUE. Don't rush things, please. Give us time to get to know each other and be sure that the right feelings are there. You can't have a perfect union without right feelings.

THOMAS. I've got them already. Why delay?

ANGÉLIQUE. It may have been easy for you, sir, but, well, your own merits don't quite, well, leap out and hit one in the face, at least not mine.

ARGAN. Oh, that. Plenty of time for that after you're married.

ANGÉLIQUE. Please, father, please, I need time. Marriage is a once-in-a-lifetime thing, nobody should be forced into it. If Mr Lillicrap is a real gentleman, he won't want someone who's marrying him against her will.

THOMAS. Non sequitur. I can be a gentleman and at the same time agree to accept your hand from your father.

ANGÉLIQUE. How can you try to get someone to love you by force and pressure? It's immoral!

THOMAS. If you read Classical literature, you'll find that the custom was to take intended brides away from their fathers' houses by force, so as to give the impression that they weren't falling into some man's arms out of choice.

ANGÉLIQUE. Ancient writers are ancient. We belong to our own times. Now. We don't need to play these silly games. When a marriage is an attractive prospect, we know perfectly well how to say yes. Why put pressure on us? There's no need. Be patient for a while. If you love me, you should want what I want.

THOMAS. I quite agree. But only where there's no conflict with the requirements of my own position. My love, I mean.

ANGÉLIQUE. But surely the best proof of love is to put the woman you love first. Me.

THOMAS. Two remarks, if you permit. Primo: I concede your point in respect of all matters outside a husband's ownership of his wife. But, secundo: a husband has an absolute right to possession of the said wife.

TOINETTE. Don't waste your breath, honestly. The gentleman has had the benefit of higher education. He'll run rings round you, always. Anyway, why not accept gracefully? You could bask in the reflected glory of being a doctor's appendage.

BÉLINE. Perhaps Angélique has someone else in mind?

ANGÉLIQUE. If I had, madame, it would be an honest and sincere choice.

ARGAN. Excuse me. Would you like a referee?

BÉLINE. In your shoes, my sweet, I wouldn't force her into this marriage. I know what I'd do instead.

ANGÉLIQUE. I know exactly what you have in mind, madame, just as I know how you feel towards me. But your advice may get turned down.

BÉLINE. Clever, educated girls like you don't care these days if they obey their fathers or not. It was different in my day.

ANGÉLIQUE. A daughter's duty goes only so far, madame. There are some demands which can simply not be met.

BÉLINE. What you mean is that you're willing to get married but you insist on choosing your husband yourself.

ANGÉLIQUE. If my father won't give me a husband I like, then at least let me plead with him not to force on me one I can't stand.

ARGAN. Gentlemen, do please excuse all this.

ANGÉLIQUE. Everyone has their individual reasons for marrying. For me, I want to marry a man I can love truly and properly for the rest of my life. Yes, I confess, I want to choose him myself, with great care. Other women may look to marriage as an escape from their parents. All they want is freedom to do exactly as they please. There are some women, madame, who consider marriage solely in terms of financial gain. They marry one old wreck after another just to gather in their inheritances. As matter-of-fact as that. No irrelevances like feelings. Money, just money makes their world go around.

BÉLINE. You're rather argumentative today, young lady. I'm not too sure what you're trying to imply.

ANGÉLIQUE. Imply? Nothing. I'm saying what I think.

BÉLINE. Well, you're making no sense at all, and I don't think we need detain you any longer.

ANGÉLIQUE. If you're trying to provoke me, it won't work. I shan't give you the pleasure. I shall count to ten.

BÉLINE. I don't have to put up with this impertinence.

ANGÉLIQUE. Excuse me, madame, I've only got to three.

BÉLINE. You're full of stupid pride, impertinence, arrogance. The whole world will turn its back on you.

ANGÉLIQUE. This will get us nowhere. I'm going to go on behaving calmly and rationally, whatever you may say or do. You want to put me in a straitjacket? You'll have to catch me first.

ARGAN. You listen here, my girl, I'm not going to argue with you. The choice is clear. Either you marry this young man, or I put you in a convent. Understand? You've got precisely four days to decide. (*To* BÉLINE.) Don't worry yourself, she'll see sense.

BÉLINE. I hate to leave you, my sugar, but I have urgent business in town. It won't wait. Back soon.

ARGAN. Off you go now, and don't forget your visit to the notary. You know why.

BÉLINE. Bye bye, chicken.

ARGAN. Bye bye, treasure . . . Now there's a woman who knows the meaning of love. I can hardly believe my luck.

DR LILLICRAP. Monsieur Argan, if you'll excuse us, we'll take our leave as well.

ARGAN. Umm, before you go, you couldn't just give me a check-up? A teeny weeny examination?

DR LILLICRAP (*taking his pulse*). Come along, Thomas, take Monsieur Argan's other wrist. See if you can do an accurate diagnosis . . . And your verdict?

THOMAS. I'd say the sick gentleman's sick pulse is the pulse of a sick man.

DR LILLICRAP. Ah, quod erat demonstrandum.

THOMAS. I'd say the pulse is pulsating a touch impulsively. We've caught it in flagrante.

DR LILLICRAP. Very good.

THOMAS. Enough élan vital to repulse my finger.

DR LILLICRAP. Bene.

THOMAS. The beat is even a mite compulsive.

DR LILLICRAP. Melius.

THOMAS. Which indicates, ipso facto, sound cardiac propulsion. There is, however, an imbalance in the splenetic parenchyma, videlicet, the spleen.

DR LILLICRAP. Optime.

ARGAN. But Dr Purgeon says it's my liver.

DR LILLICRAP. Well, naturally, he would. But remember, the parenchyma and the liver are fundamentally the same thing. That's because they are cognatively connected by means of the vas breve, the pylorus, and even in certain circumstances, the meatus cholidichi . . . Dr Purgeon has doubtless told you to eat plenty of roast beef?

ARGAN. No, boiled. Boiled beef.

DR LILLICRAP. Obviously. Boiled, roast, it's the same thing. He's an excellent doctor, you couldn't ask for better. He knows what he's doing.

ARGAN. Doctor, how many grains of salt should I put on my egg?

DR LILLICRAP. Six, eight, ten, but always even numbers. It's the same with drops and pills, except that they must always be odd numbers.

ARGAN. Gentlemen, I bid you good day.

7. BÉLINE, ARGAN.

BÉLINE. I thought I'd better have a quick word with you, my little object of desire, before going out. Only I think you should be warned. I was passing Angélique's room and I caught a glimpse of a young man who disappeared when he saw I'd spotted him.

ARGAN. A man with my daughter!

BÉLINE. Exactly. Her little sister Louison was with them. She might be able to tell you more.

ARGAN. Fetch her, my love, fetch her this instant. Ah! What a schemer! No wonder she won't obey me. I see it all now.

8. LOUISON, ARGAN.

LOUISON. Hello papa. Step-mamma said you want to see me. Why, papa?

ARGAN. Come over here. Come on. Here. That's it. Turn round. Look at me. So?

LOUISON. What, papa?

ARGAN. Eh?

LOUISON. What do you mean?

ARGAN. Haven't you got something to tell me?

LOUISON. If you want, I can recite the story of the Ass's Skin, or the Fable of The Crow and The Fox. I've just learnt them.

ARGAN. No, that's not what I want to hear.

LOUISON. What then?

ARGAN. Little fox! You know exactly what I mean.

LOUISON. I don't, papa.

ARGAN. Is this how you obey and respect your father?

LOUISON. What do you mean?

ARGAN. Haven't I said you must always come and tell me everything you see?

LOUISON. Yes, papa.

ARGAN. And have you?

LOUISON. Yes, papa. I've come and told you everything I've seen.

ARGAN. And have you seen anything today?

LOUISON. No, papa.

ARGAN. No?

LOUISON. No, papa.

ARGAN. You're sure?

LOUISON. I'm sure.

ARGAN. Right, now it's my turn to show you something!

He grabs a cane.

LOUISON. Oh papa, please don't!

ARGAN. So, you little adder. I haven't heard you tell me there was a man in your sister's room.

LOUISON. Papa!

ARGAN. This'll teach you to lie to me!

LOUISON. (*falling to her knees*). Oh, please, please, I'm sorry. It's Angélique's fault. She told me not to tell you, but I will, I will.

ARGAN. First, you must be caned. We'll talk after.

LOUISON. Papa, I'm sorry, truly I am.

ARGAN. Bend over.

LOUISON. Don't hurt me.

ARGAN. I will, I must.

LOUISON. Please, don't.

ARGAN (*taking hold of her*). Come on!

LOUISON. Oh papa, that hurt. I think you've killed me. (*She pretends to die*).

ARGAN. Hey! Louison! Wake up! My little girl, my Louison! Oh God, what have I done? Damn cane! Stupid cane! Louison, darling! Louison, Louison!

LOUISON. Shhh, there there, papa, I'm not a hundred per cent dead.

ARGAN. What? You crafty thing! All right, I'll let you off so long as you tell me everything you know. Is that fair?

LOUISON. Oh yes.

ARGAN. But remember: this little finger knows everything and it'll tell me the moment you start lying again.

LOUISON. Please, papa, please don't tell Angélique I told.

ARGAN. I won't. Promise.

LOUISON. What happened is that a man came into her room when I was there.

ARGAN. And?

LOUISON. I said, 'Can I help you?', and he said he was Angélique's music teacher.

ARGAN. Did he, indeed? Then what?

LOUISON. Angélique said, 'Please leave, please, please! Oh, you'll be the death of me!'

ARGAN. And?

LOUISON. He wouldn't leave.

ARGAN. What did he say to her?

LOUISON. Lots and lots of things.

ARGAN. What else happened?

LOUISON. He went on saying things, like how he had these feelings about her, and how she was the most beautiful girl he'd ever seen in his whole life.

ARGAN. Then what?

LOUISON. He knelt down in front of her.

ARGAN. Then what?

LOUISON. He started kissing her hands.

ARGAN. Then what?

LOUISON. Step-mamma came to the door, so he went out quickly.

ARGAN. Anything else?

LOUISON. No, papa.

ARGAN. Now then, this little finger's twitching. I think it wants to tell me something. (*Puts his finger to his ear.*) Yes? Ah? Oh! Really? Really! My little finger says you've left something out.

LOUISON. Papa, your little finger's telling fibs.

ARGAN. Careful!

LOUISON. No, papa, honestly. It's fibbing, don't believe a word it says.

ARGAN. We'll see. Off you go now, but be careful. Run along . . . Ah, children aren't children any more. What a business! I haven't been able to concentrate on my illness in all this. I'm drained. (*Falls into his chair*).

9. BÉRALDE, ARGAN.

BÉRALDE. Greetings, Argan. And how's my one and only brother today?

ARGAN. Bad.

BÉRALDE. How d'you mean, bad?

ARGAN. I'm so weak . . .

BÉRALDE. That's terrible.

ARGAN. Scarcely strength to speak.

BÉRALDE. Argan, I think I've found a solution to this Angélique business.

ARGAN (*suddenly energetic and angry, getting up from his chair*). Don't mention that name to me! You know what she is, don't you? There's a word for it, but I shan't soil my mouth. She's going into a convent in the next forty-eight hours.

BÉRALDE. That's the spirit! I'm delighted to see you've re-covered a bit. Glad my visit's cheered you up. We'll speak about serious things in a moment. But first, I thought you might like to meet some theatre folk I ran into today. They're a bit . . . unexpected, but very entertaining. They'll take your mind off things. Just hear them. Songs, dances. I'm sure ten minutes with them is worth a cupboard-ful of Dr Purgeon's pills and potions. What do you say?

Second Interlude

Argan's brother brings on several Egyptians in Moorish costume, to entertain him with a mixture of songs and dance.

1st MOORISH WOMAN.
    Gather rosebuds while you may.
    Youth must decay.
    The time for love is now.

    Without passion's bright flame,
    Life's an empty game.
    The time for love is now.
    Gather rosebuds while you may.
    Youth must decay.
    The time for love is now.

    The sun's shining, make hay!
    Good looks go,
    Liver-spots grow,
    Beauty won't stay,
    We all decay.

    Make hay, you'll soon forget how!
    Gather rosebuds while you may.
    Youth must decay.
    The time for love is now.

2nd MOORISH WOMAN.
    What is this thing called love?
    It's so urgent when we're young.

It's ready, steady, go!
Who ever says no?
Yet we're told all the time
It's a sin, a crime.
We're young, let's have the pleasure.
After, we'll have time to count the cost,
Repent at leisure.

3rd MOORISH WOMAN.
I feel charming,
He's disarming,
He can be my lover . . .
Now, he's had his wicked way
There's a price to pay.
It's the same the whole world over.

4th MOORISH WOMAN.
They steal inside our clothes,
And then steal out again.
But the stealing I loathe,
The theft that causes most pain,
It's when they steal our heart,
Every time they steal our heart.

2nd MOORISH WOMAN.
How can we recognise
A lurking Don Juan?

4th MOORISH WOMAN.
We've known lots already.
We've had masses to chew on.

ALL. No, we can't fight it.
Oh, the delight it

Is to touch, stroke, caress,
Be touched, stroked, caressed.

Mothers, cleaners, scrubbers, cooks,
That's how our husbands define us.
Girls, while we've still got our looks,
There're others to wine us and dine us!

Overgrown children, all aches and great pains,
Their bruised shins and egos, their terrible sprains,
Their poor battered pride and their tickly throats . . .
Well, let's have no more, girls, we all want our oats!

Dance, accompanied by performing monkeys.

Act Three

1. BÉRALDE, ARGAN, TOINETTE.

BÉRALDE. So, Argan, what did you think of that? Better than pumping things up your bottom, eh?

TOINETTE. The Lillicrap solution, ha ha.

BÉRALDE. Now then, I think we should have a talk.

ARGAN. You'll have to wait a bit. I'll be back.

TOINETTE. Hey, not so fast. Remember you can't walk without a stick.

ARGAN. Oh yes.

2. BÉRALDE, TOINETTE.

TOINETTE. You won't forget to speak up for your niece, will you?

BÉRALDE. Indeed I won't. I'll do all I can for her.

TOINETTE. This lunatic marriage must be stopped at all costs. What I thought was this: let's get a doctor on our side. He could turn your brother away from that Dr Purgeon and bring him to his senses. The problem is,

I couldn't think of anyone, so I'm working on a scheme of my own.

BÉRALDE. Yes?

TOINETTE. It's a bit . . . elaborate . . . but it should be fun. And it certainly ought to work. Let me work on it. Ah, careful, he's coming back.

3.ARGAN, BÉRALDE.

BÉRALDE. Now, before we start our conversation, I want you to promise me you won't lose your temper.

ARGAN. I promise.

BÉRALDE. You'll stay cool and calm, whatever I say.

ARGAN. Promise.

BÉRALDE. We'll have a sober, rational discussion. There are important things to sort out.

ARGAN. I promise. Look, never mind the overture, Béralde. Say what you have to say.

BÉRALDE. All right. Why is it that a wealthy man like you, with only one daughter – the little one doesn't really count – can think of putting her into a convent?

ARGAN. Why is it that the head of a household has to justify himself?

BÉRALDE. Your wife doesn't miss an opportunity to tell you what a good thing it would be if you were rid of both your girls. She'd love to see them safely inside a convent.

ARGAN. Ahah, that's what it's all about! You want to drag my poor wife into it. She's the villain of the piece, don't tell me. Universal scapegoat.

BÉRALDE. Let's leave her out of it. I'm sure she has the very best of intentions for all of you. She never considers herself, she worships the ground you stand on, and her warmth and kindness to your children are legendary. Not another word about her. Let's get back to Angélique. You want her to marry a doctor's son. Where's the logic in that?

ARGAN. The logic is that I need a son-in-law who'll be useful to me.

BÉRALDE. With respect, that's scarcely relevant to your daughter. But there is another candidate, as it happens, and a much better one from her point of view.

ARGAN. Not from mine.

BÉRALDE. Who's getting married, you or her?

ARGAN. Both. In my family, I'll only tolerate people I need.

BÉRALDE. By that token, if Louison were old enough, you'd make her marry an apothecary?

ARGAN. Why not?

BÉRALDE. How long will this obsession with doctors and apothecaries go on, for heaven's sake? You want to be ill, you take no notice of your friends or of Nature itself.

ARGAN. What exactly are you implying?

BÉRALDE. I'm implying, my dear brother, that I've never seen anyone as fit as you. I'd love to have your constitution. You're in great shape. If you want proof of what I'm saying, look at the way you've stood up to all that barrage of cures, remedies and treatments.

ARGAN. But that's the point! If I didn't see Dr Purgeon every three days, I'd succumb. That's what he says.

BÉRALDE. At this rate, he'll still be looking after you in the life everlasting.

ARGAN. This is ridiculous. You don't believe in medicine, do you?

BÉRALDE. No, frankly, I don't. I don't believe that it promotes good health.

ARGAN. You refuse to believe in well-established scientific facts?

BÉRALDE. Absolutely not. I'd go even further. Between you, me and the bedpost, I'd say that medicine is one of the daftest bits of nonsense ever dreamt up by humankind. Scientific facts? Mumbo-jumbo! It's ridiculous to think one person can cure another.

ARGAN. I see. And why is that?

BÉRALDE. Human beings are too complex and enigmatic. We may want to delude ourselves, but we understand precious little. Nature didn't intend us to.

ARGAN. So, according to you, doctors know nothing?

BÉRALDE. Oh yes they do. They've got degrees, they know all the jargon, all the patter. Huge medical dictionaries.

But what they haven't got is any way of making people better. Lilicrap admitted this

ARGAN. They still get nearer than the rest of us.

BÉRALDE. What they're expert at is frightening us. Latin and Greek words as long as a waiting-list. Always promises, never results.

ARGAN. Rubbish. There are some people in medicine today, every bit as clever as you. In any case, if all doctors were useless, nobody would see them, would they?

BÉRALDE. I'm afraid that says more about human gullibility than anything else.

ARGAN. But doctors must believe what they're doing is right, since they do it to themselves.

BÉRALDE. Some of them are stupid enough to believe in it, like their patients. And they do nicely out of it, thank you very much. Others make a packet without believing a single word. Your Dr Purgeon is in the former camp. A no-bones sort of doctor, uncomplicated as you like, who's swallowed the lot, hook, line and sinker. He'd go to the stake rather than take an objective look at medical 'truth'. For him, medicine's about certainties, certainties and . . . certainties. He's coarse, he's blunt, he's blind, and he doesn't care. He goes around sticking needles in here, enemas there, as if there were no tomorrow. You can't really hold it against him, it's not malice on his part. But he'll finish you off in the absolute conviction he's doing wonders for you. No cloud of self-doubt will ever darken the sky of his complacency. It's not only his patients; he'd just as cheerfully despatch his wife, his children, himself even.

ARGAN. You don't like him, do you? Tell me, what should people do when they're ill?

BÉRALDE. Nothing.

ARGAN. Nothing?

BÉRALDE. Nothing. Rest, let Nature take its course. Nature sorts things out. It's our impatience, our anxiety, which wreck everything. Most people die of cures, not illnesses.

ARGAN. Oh, surely you'd concede that Nature can be helped along?

BÉRALDE. No, people like to hang on to comforting ideas and fantasies because it's soothing. But because something's soothing doesn't mean it's true. Doctors'll tell you how they help Nature, encourage it, speed it up, restore the balance, get everything working again. They'll go on and on about thin blood, thick blood, lower bowel, upper bowel, here a gland, there a gland, everywhere a quack quack. And what are they really doing? I'll tell you. They're quoting from the Collected Novels, Short Stories and Fairy Tales of that fertile old hack called Medicine. Visit your local bookshop, look under 'F' for Fiction . . . dreams, doctors are pedlars of dreams. And when you wake up from a dream, too often you wish you hadn't had it in the first place.

ARGAN. I bow to your superior knowledge and wisdom. Of course you know more than all the doctors put together.

BÉRALDE. Hear doctors pronounce, their intelligence is off the end of the scale. But watch them at work, they haven't got a single clue.

ARGAN. Oh, you're too clever for me. I wish one of these poor useless doctors were here to defend himself. He'd put you in your place, like that.

BÉRALDE. I'm not interested. Let people go on thinking what they want. This conversation was for our ears only. But I'd love to open your eyes, even so. Look, there's a comedy by Molière on at the moment. That would explain better than I can.

ARGAN. Molière! One of those arty-farty people. He's got no business making fun of medicine. It's far too serious.

BÉRALDE. He's not mocking medicine. It's the abuse of it he finds laughable.

ARGAN. He still shouldn't stick his oar in. He's no right to ridicule his betters. Medicine's not the right subject for a night out at the theatre.

BÉRALDE. But what else can he put on stage except what humans do? You see plenty of plays about kings and queens. So why not doctors?

ARGAN. Dammit, if I were a doctor, I'd soon sort out that Molière. I'd let him die slowly if he were ill. He could plead for medicines, treatment, but let him whistle. 'Die, go on, die,' I'd say, 'another time you'll know better than to make fun of these . . . these saints'.

BÉRALDE. You have got it for him!

ARGAN. He's a fool, and he's dangerous. Doctors would do well to take my advice.

BÉRALDE. I'm sure he'd outsmart your doctors. He'd never seek their help.

ARGAN. He'd be the one to suffer.

BÉRALDE. He says you need to be as strong as an ox to fight off both an illness and its cure. For his part, he's only got enough resistance for the illness.

ARGAN. Bizarre logic! Look, we must stop this. My pulse is going wild again.

BÉRALDE. Right, agreed. Let's talk of something else. I really don't think you can shut your daughter up in a convent simply because she's fighting one of your batty schemes. It's really going too far. Surely a woman has the right to choose her husband? After all, it's for life, and it's Angélique who's doing the marrying, not you.

4. MR FLORID *carrying a syringe,* ARGAN, BÉRALDE.

ARGAN. Ah, Béralde, excuse me one moment.

BÉRALDE. What's the matter?

ARGAN. I've got to take something for my bowels. Mr Florid specialises in bowel disorders.

BÉRALDE. Are you completely crazy? Can't one single moment pass without an enema or a sedative or some damn pill? Please, just this once, say no. What about tomorrow?

ARGAN. Mr Florid, what about this evening or tomorrow morning?

MR FLORID (*to* BÉRALDE). I must ask Monsieur not to interfere. I know what I'm doing. Monsieur does not. Keep out of this.

BÉRALDE (*pointing to his own face*). With the greatest respect, Monsieur, this is a face you're addressing, not a backside. A little common courtesy, if you please.

MR FLORID. You're wasting my time. You can't play around with medical people like this. The attitude in this house is frivolous, and I shall report back to Dr Purgeon that I was prevented from following his instructions. You'll hear more of this . . . (*Exits*).

ARGAN. I don't think he's pleased.

BÉRALDE. What a tragedy, refusing Purgeon's laxative. No, Argan, you've got to get over this love affair you're having with medicine. It's beyond a joke.

ARGAN. It's easy for you, you're not sick. I wish you were in my shoes, you'd soon change your tune.

BÉRALDE. What exactly is it that's wrong with you?

ARGAN. What's wrong? What's wrong! Béralde, sometimes I wonder about you . . . Ah, here's Dr Purgeon.

5. DR PURGEON, ARGAN, BÉRALDE, TOINETTE.

DR PURGEON. What's this I've just been hearing? You won't take my prescriptions, you're laughing at my diagnoses?

ARGAN. Doctor, it's not . . .

DR PURGEON. And what gives a patient the right to question his doctor?

TOINETTE. It's an outrage.

DR PURGEON. I took great pains making up that enema.

ARGAN. Not my fault.

DR PURGEON. I used the best formula. Tried and tested.

TOINETTE. Beneath contempt.

DR PURGEON. You'd have had blissful bowels.

ARGAN. Béralde . . .

DR PURGEON. Sending my man packing like that!

ARGAN. It was Béralde.

DR PURGEON. Quite unforgivable.

TOINETTE. Straight from the horse's mouth.

DR PURGEON. You're out to . . . to murder medicine.

ARGAN. My brother . . .

DR PURGEON. It's . . . civil disobedience.

TOINETTE. Not lèse majesty, lèse quackery.

DR PURGEON. I'll have to strike you off my list.

ARGAN. It was my brother.

DR PURGEON. I want nothing more to do with you.

TOINETTE. Very wise.

DR PURGEON. I'm winding everything up, including the deed of covenant I took out for my nephew as his wedding gift. (*Tears up a deed.*)

ARGAN. It's all my brother's fault.

DR PURGEON. Spurn my suppositories!

ARGAN. Please bring them back, I'll take the lot!

DR PURGEON. I'd have seen to you once and for all.

TOINETTE. He doesn't deserve it.

DR PURGEON. I'd have irrigated everything, left your insides squeaky clean.

ARGAN. Ah, Béralde!

DR PURGEON. It would only have needed a dozen or so bottles for a perfect evacuation.

TOINETTE. He's not worthy of such attention.

DR PURGEON. Still, as you obviously don't wish me to be the one . . .

ARGAN. It's not my fault.

DR PURGEON. As all the time you were the dark angel rebelling against his Father . . .

TOINETTE. This must be punished.

DR PURGEON. As you've committed the sin of disobedience . . .

ARGAN. No, I haven't, no!

DR PURGEON. All I say to you is that I cast you adrift, I abandon you to your boiling arteries, your stinking entrails,

your filthy blood, your sour bile, your puffy skin, your
starchy flesh, your corrupt, evil body!

TOINETTE. Well done.

ARGAN. Oh, my God!

DR PURGEON. And I hope that in less than a week your
illness becomes terminal.

ARGAN. God, help me!

DR PURGEON. That you fall into bradepepsia.

ARGAN. Doctor!

DR PURGEON. From bradepepsia into dyspepsia.

ARGAN. Doctor!

DR PURGEON. From dyspepsia into apepsia.

ARGAN. Doctor Purgeon!

DR PURGEON. From apepsia into diarrhoea.

ARGAN. Doctor!

DR PURGEON. From diarrhoea into dysentery.

ARGAN. Doctor!

DR PURGEON. From dysentry into dropsy.

ARGAN. Doctor Purgeon!

DR PURGEON. And from dropsy into the complete and
utter extinction of your life! Hanging's too good for you!

6. ARGAN, BÉRALDE.

ARGAN. Oh, Béralde, I've had it, I'm done for. And it's all your fault.

BÉRALDE. Let's not exaggerate.

ARGAN. It's the end. Medicine is avenged.

BÉRALDE. Frankly, you're off your head. I wish with every bone in my body that you'd snap out of this. Get a grip. Think straight. Stop letting your imagination get the better of you.

ARGAN. Did you hear him, though? Those terrible illnesses I'm certain to get?

BÉRALDE. Are you that naïve?

ARGAN. I've got less than a week to live, he said.

BÉRALDE. He isn't God. He can't shorten or lengthen your life at a stroke. Your life's in your own hands, no-one else's. Dr Purgeon's anger won't kill you, any more than his medicines will keep you alive. I'd have thought this experience would turn you against doctors forever. If you refuse to change your ways, at least find someone who's less of a tyrant.

ARGAN. But Dr Purgeon knows me inside out. He knows exactly what to do.

BÉRALDE. Sometimes I don't have the faintest idea how you see the world. Are you wearing the right glasses?

7. TOINETTE, ARGAN, BÉRALDE.

TOINETTE. Sir, there's a doctor here, says he wants to see you.

ARGAN. Which doctor?

TOINETTE. Not a witch doctor, a proper one.

ARGAN. What's his name?

TOINETTE. Don't know. Funnily enough, he's the spitting image of yours truly. I know my mother's been the model widow since her old man passed away, but, well, it makes you wonder.

ARGAN. Show him in.

BÉRALDE. Your dream's come true. Out goes one doctor, in comes another.

ARGAN. You've really put the cat among the pigeons, haven't you!

BÉRALDE. Don't start again.

ARGAN. I can't stop thinking about those hundreds of undiagnosed complaints I've got. IRONY

8. TOINETTE *disguised as doctor*, ARGAN, BÉRALDE.

TOINETTE. Good day to you. Thank you for agreeing to see me. Allow me to offer you my varied and expert services. I can do you an excellent blood-letting, nice and smooth, or

I've a wide range of purgatives, including the very latest on the market.

ARGAN. How kind . . . But this is Toinette's double.

TOINETTE. One moment, sir, if you don't mind. I must pop out to tell my personal assistant something. Back in two shakes of a wooden leg.

ARGAN. It is Toinette.

BÉRALDE. A striking resemblance, I grant you. But these things happen.

ARGAN. It's amazing.

9. TOINETTE, ARGAN, BÉRALDE.

TOINETTE (*she has taken off her doctor's gown so quickly that it is difficult to believe she was a doctor a moment ago*). Yes, sir?

ARGAN. Pardon?

TOINETTE. Didn't you call?

ARGAN. No.

TOINETTE. Sorry, must be hearing things.

ARGAN. Now you're here, you can see just how much you look like this new doctor.

TOINETTE (*leaving*). Yes, yes. I'm busy. I've seen all I want to see of him.

ARGAN. If I hadn't seen them separately, I'd say they were one and the same person.

BÉRALDE. There's quite a substantial literature on this phenomenon. Even the experts have been fooled.

ARGAN. Well, I'd have been fooled by this pair. I'd have sworn they were the same person.

10. TOINETTE *disguised as doctor*, ARGAN, BÉRALDE.

TOINETTE. My apologies.

ARGAN. Unbelievable.

TOINETTE. I hope you'll forgive my curiosity, but I wanted to see for myself this incredibly famous invalid. Your reputation stretches far and wide.

ARGAN. This is a great pleasure for me, sir.

TOINETTE. Why are you staring at me like that? Wondering about my age? How old do you think?

ARGAN. Oh, twenty-six, twenty-seven.

TOINETTE. Ahah! Ninety.

ARGAN. Ninety?

TOINETTE. Ninety. That's one effect of my medical skills, to stay permanently young and lively.

ARGAN. Well indeed, what a fine . . . geriatric!

TOINETTE. No, no. Not geriatric. Peripatetic. I wander from town to town, district to district, bringing my gifts to a public who might not otherwise get the benefit. I sniff out illnesses worthy of my concern, the complicated, mysterious ones, none of your common-or-garden colds, aches and pains, rheumatism, migraine, athlete's foot. No, I want the big ones, raging fevers for weeks on end, wild delirium. I want plagues, dropsy, pleurisy, collapsed and/or missing lungs, that kind of thing. I'd really love it, sir, if you were suffering from any combination of all these, even better if you were at death's door, the despair of every ordinary doctor, so that I could take charge and get to work with my remarkable cures. Oh, how I could sort you out!

ARGAN. Thanks very much.

TOINETTE. Give me your hand, let's check this naughty little pulse, shall we? Ahah, ahah, oh dear, oh dear me, not good, not right at all. But we'll soon have you ticking properly. It's a cheeky little pulse, got a will of its own. Settle, settle! Down boy! You mustn't be afraid of me. (*To* ARGAN.) Who's your doctor?

ARGAN. Dr Purgeon.

TOINETTE. Can't say I know him. Hasn't made any sort of a name for himself. What does he say's wrong with you?

ARGAN. He says it's my liver. The others say it's spleen.

TOINETTE. Amateurs! Lungs, that what it is. Lungs.

ARGAN. Lungs?

TOINETTE. Lungs. What are your symptoms?

ARGAN. Headaches.

TOINETTE. Exactly. Lungs.

ARGAN. Sometimes my eyes feel all swimmy.

TOINETTE. Lungs.

ARGAN. Then again I feel sick.

TOINETTE. Lungs.

ARGAN. My legs give way.

TOINETTE. Lungs.

ARGAN. My stomach aches.

TOINETTE. Lungs. Do you have a hearty appetite?

ARGAN. Yes, doctor.

TOINETTE. Lungs. Do you enjoy an occasional drink or two?

ARGAN. Yes, doctor.

TOINETTE. Lungs. Do you take forty winks of an
    afternoon?

ARGAN. Yes, doctor.

TOINETTE. Lungs, no question. What food does your
    doctor recommend?

ARGAN. Soup.

TOINETTE. Fool.

ARGAN. Breast of chicken.

TOINETTE. Idiot.

ARGAN. Veal cutlets.

TOINETTE. Cretin.

ARGAN. Meat broth.

TOINETTE. Charlatan.

ARGAN. New-laid eggs, chicken or duck.

TOINETTE. Quack. *mockery.*

ARGAN. And last thing at night, stewed prunes. Regularly.

TOINETTE. Moron.

ARGAN. And, most important he says I must always water down my wine.

TOINETTE. Ignoramus maximus crapulous! He's suffering from what us doctors called stupidity. You have to take your drink neat. Your blood needs thickening. What you need is generous helpings of roast beef, thick bacon rashers, a good selection of dairy produce, cheeses, porridge, oatmeal, rice puddings, chestnuts, pancakes, that sort of thing. You need to clot that watery blood. Your doctor's on another planet. I'll send one of my partners round, he'll keep an eye on you for the duration of my stay.

ARGAN. I'd be most grateful.

TOINETTE. What's wrong with that arm?

ARGAN. I beg your pardon.

TOINETTE. I'd have it amputated this minute, if I were you.

ARGAN. Why?

TOINETTE. Can't you see it's hogging all the nourishment and making the other shrivel up?

ARGAN. But I need both arms.

TOINETTE. Oh dear, now that right eye, I'd have it surgically removed without delay.

ARGAN. Lose an eye!

TOINETTE. Can't you see it's a parasite? It's stealing all the other one's sustenance. Believe me, have it whipped out, and you'll see a whole lot better out of the left one.

ARGAN. Could I have a second opinion?

TOINETTE. Sorry, must dash. Got an important meeting. We're discussing the treatment for a patient who died yesterday.

ARGAN. A patient who died?

TOINETTE. Indeed. We want to determine what we should have done to save him. Good day.

ARGAN. Do you mind seeing yourself out? I'm not feeling so good.

BÉRALDE. Now that doctor seemed pretty much on the ball to me.

ARGAN. But he's so hasty in his conclusions.

BÉRALDE. All specialists are the same.

ARGAN. I don't know, cut off my arm, remove an eye for the sake of the others! What sort of medical ethics is that? I think I prefer to let them muddle along as they are!

11. TOINETTE, ARGAN, BÉRALDE.

TOINETTE (*off-stage*). All right, all right, no funny business. I won't, that's all, I just won't.

ARGAN. Won't what?

TOINETTE. Won't have my pulse taken by that doctor, dirty old man.

ARGAN. Is that what he was doing? At ninety?

BÉRALDE. Changing the subject, Argan, I think we should talk about my niece. Now that you've fallen out with Purgeon, there's another offer we should consider.

ARGAN. No, I've told you, she's earned a convent and that's what she's getting. How dare she oppose me? I fancy there's some love affair at the bottom of this. You may think I don't notice certain things, but I do.

BÉRALDE. All right, and what if there is a little matter of mutual affection, is that so criminal? Why are you so furious? It would be prefectly normal if it led to marriage.

ARGAN. Be that as it may, she's going into the convent, and that's that.

BÉRALDE. This isn't about Angélique, is it? Someone else is behind this.

ARGAN. Ah, I know what you're driving at. My wife. She gets up your nose, doesn't she?

BÉRALDE. Your words, not mine. But yes, it is your wife I mean. I have to say that you're as blind and stubborn about her as you are about medicine. You fall into every trap she sets, and I can't bear to see it.

TOINETTE. Oh, Monsieur Béralde, you shouldn't talk about madame like that. If ever a woman loved her husband deeply and sincerely, it's madame . . . You shouldn't say such things!

ARGAN. Tell him how affectionate she can be.

TOINETTE. Oh yes.

ARGAN. How my illness is upsetting her.

TOINETTE. Oh yes.

ARGAN. All those little kindnesses.

TOINETTE. Oh yes. (*To* BÉRALDE.) Shall I show you how much she loves him? Do you want to see for yourself? (*To* ARGAN.) Let's show him.

ARGAN. Now what are you up to?

TOINETTE. Madame will be back any moment. Slump down in the chair, pretend you're dead. We'll soon see how devastated she is when she hears the news.

ARGAN. Well, if you say so.

TOINETTE (*To* BÉRALDE). You hide over there.

ARGAN. Is it . . . life-threatening to pretend to be dead?

TOINETTE. No, no, of course it isn't. Go on, stretch out. (*Whispers.*) We'll enjoy showing your brother up. Here she comes.

12. BÉLINE, TOINETTE, ARGAN, BÉRALDE.

TOINETTE. Oh, my God! Help! Something's happened.

BÉLINE. What is it, Toinette?

TOINETTE. Oh, madame!

BÉLINE. What on earth's the matter?

TOINETTE. Your husband's dead.

BÉLINE. Dead?

TOINETTE. Dead. The poor man's dead.

BÉLINE. Are you sure?

TOINETTE. Absolutely certain. I was here on my own with
him, and he just passed away in my arms. Look at him
there, in that chair.

BÉLINE. Heaven be praised! At last I'm rid of him. Stupid
great lump! Cheer up, Toinette, it's a relief all round.

TOINETTE. I thought, madame, we might actually cry.

BÉLINE. Cry? No, no, no. Frankly, who's going to miss him?
What a futile existence! A pain, a nuisance to everyone. A
disgusting, smelly carcass. Those endless purges, those pills,
those syrups. All that moaning. Beyond endurance, believe
me. Blowing his nose, coughing, spitting and worse.

TOINETTE. What a touching obituary.

BÉLINE. I've got a plan, Toinette, and you must help me.
You won't go away empty-handed. Does anyone know yet
that the old boy's dead? Good. Let's get him into his bed,
and keep things quiet for the moment. We'll play for time.

I need to get my hands on his papers and his money. I won't have spent the best years of my life in this living hell for nothing. Come on, Toinette, let's find his keys.

ARGAN (*getting up suddenly*). Just one moment, if you don't mind.

BÉLINE. Aah!

ARGAN. So, wife, this is what you call love?

TOINETTE. Ah! Oh! The corpse isn't dead.

ARGAN. (*to Béline as she leaves*). I'm moved by the depth of your feelings for me. And I'm delighted I didn't miss your touching little eulogy. You've certainly taught me a few things. I'll be very different from now on.

BÉRALDE (*emerging from his hiding-place*). So, Argan, what do you make of that?

TOINETTE. Who would have thought! But I can hear Angélique. Get back in that chair like you were before. Let's see how she takes your death. It's not a bad idea to find out what the whole family thinks while we're about it.

13. ANGÉLIQUE, ARGAN, TOINETTE, BÉRALDE.

TOINETTE. Oh, no, no, no! This is the worst day of my life!

ANGÉLIQUE. What's the matter, Toinette?

TOINETTE. Very bad news.

ANGÉLIQUE. What? What news?

TOINETTE. Your father's dead.

ANGÉLIQUE. Dead?

TOINETTE. Dead. There. Look. In that chair. He suddenly went all faint, and that was that.

ANGÉLIQUE. Oh my God! My heavens! It can't be true, it can't be! This is awful. I can't bear it. He was all I had in the world, he was still angry with me when he . . . when he . . . I'll never forgive myself! I want to die! Oh, papa, papa!

14. CLÉANTE, ANGÉLIQUE, ARGAN, TOINETTE, BÉRALDE.

CLÉANTE. My Angélique, what's happened? Why are you like this?

ANGÉLIQUE. I've lost the dearest thing in my life. I've lost my father.

CLÉANTE. Oh, what a dreadful thing! What a terrible shock! I was coming here to introduce myself to him, now that he'd heard about me from your uncle. I was hoping I'd convince him, that he'd see I was serious about marrying you.

ANGÉLIQUE. Cléante, we can't think about any of that now. No more talk of marriage, please. I can't, not now. I'll do what he wanted, and go into a convent. Papa, I'll try to make up for everything, just a little. I promise. Please, please, try to forgive me just a little bit.

ARGAN. Ah, my little girl.

ANGÉLIQUE. Aah!

ARGAN. Come closer, don't be frightened. I'm not dead. You are my flesh and blood. You are real. I'm so glad I've seen who you really are, so full of natural goodness.

ANGÉLIQUE. Oh, papa, papa, I don't understand any of this, but it doesn't matter, it's wonderful you're back. A miracle. Can I ask you just one favour? If you won't let me marry Cléante, please don't make me marry anyone else. That's the only thing I'll ever ask.

CLÉANTE (falling to his knees). Please sir, please listen to two people who are desperately in love. Listen to us both.

BÉRALDE. So, Argan, how long are you going to hold out?

TOINETTE. All this love, doesn't it give you even the tiniest warm feeling in the tummy?

ARGAN. I'll agree . . . If . . . he becomes a doctor. Yes, let him become a doctor, and they can get married.

CLÉANTE. Willingly. If that's all that's needed to become your son-in-law, I'll do it. I'll become anything you want, apothecary, anything. You name it, I'll become it.

BÉRALDE. I've just had a thought, Argan. Why don't you become a doctor yourself? Patient and healer, one and the same person? Much more convenient.

TOINETTE. What a brilliant idea! You'll always recover. Guaranteed. What illness would be fool enough to stand up to a doctor?

ARGAN. Might you possibly be laughing at me? Anyway, I'm too old to start studying.

BÉRALDE. Studying, that's just a word. You're as clever as any student. I'd go so far as to say most of them are less intelligent than you.

ARGAN. But I don't know any of the language, all that Latin and Greek. I'd have to learn thousands of illnesses and cures.

BÉRALDE. That'll come, as soon as you put on cap and gown.

ARGAN. As soon as?

BÉRALDE. As soon as. A nice long gown, headgear to go with it, and the whole world will believe anything you say. Make it up as you go along, they'll worship you.

TOINETTE. What about a neat beard? Very distinguished. With the right beard, you're half-way there.

CLÉANTE. For me, I'm game, whatever you all decide.

BÉRALDE. Shall we do it now?

ARGAN. What, straightaway?

BÉRALDE. Why not? Here, now.

ARGAN. Here? In this house?

BÉRALDE. I've got a friend who knows some people in the School of Medicine. I'm sure they could be here in two minutes, perform the ceremony. It won't cost you a penny.

ARGAN. What must I do? Are there special things I have to say?

BÉRALDE. They'll tell you. It's easy. You'll have your lines written down for you. Go and get ready, and I'll fetch them.

ARGAN. All right. I'll get ready.

CLÉANTE. What have you got in mind? Who exactly are these friends of yours?

TOINETTE. Yes, do explain.

BÉRALDE. Shall we have a bit of fun tonight? We deserve it. Apparently there's a theatre company here who've been rehearsing a piece about a man who's just passed his medical exams. It's a whole ceremony, with music and dancing. I thought we could all have a part in it, with my brother starring as the doctor.

ANGÉLIQUE. Don't you think you're sending my poor father up a bit too much?

BÉRALDE. Not sending him up: indulging his fantasy. Anyway, don't give it away. We can all have some innocent fun, no harm in that. It is carnival time. So, let's get everything ready.

CLÉANTE (to ANGÉLIQUE). Is this all right?

ANGÉLIQUE. I suppose so, if uncle says so.

Third Interlude

A burlesque ceremony to instal a new doctor, in words, music and dance.

The scene-shifters organise the stage accompanied by music. Then enter the whole gathering, comprising eight syringe-bearers, six apothecaries, twenty-two doctors, and the candidate with ten surgeons, eight dancing and two singing. All take up their places, allotted by rank.

PRESIDENT. Distinguissimi doctores,
    Molto learnèd professores,
    Sumus gathered here today
    To welcome our new protégé.
    Will you each please raise your glass!
    Drink! In vitro veritas!
    Remember our motto,
    Before you get blotto . . .
    'Per laxativa ad astra,
    Totum scrotum est'.
    Personally dicto,
    I've huge admiratio
    For our respected professio.
    Let us recall, ergo,
    The words of our logo . . .
    'Mens sauna in corpore sano'.

    For medecina there's a vogue now,
    No doctor's quack or cheat or rogue now,
    We state the cure; you'd better heed it.
    You've got the cash, and don't we need it!
    The whole world likes to babble bunkum,

The sick, let's kick 'em up the rectum.
We own the mundus, look, we're gods,
We cure all ills with sennapods.

For omnes nos, necesse est
To do our constant, level best,
To tell the kind of stories
That win us new doctores.
Take note of our motto
Before you get blotto . . .
'Clever descriptions, unheard-of ills,
Expensive prescriptions, enormous great bills'.

Now standing here before us
Monsieur Argan, who adores us.
Hey presto, hocus pocus,
He'll join our magnum opus.
Our feeling's pro, not anti.
Rise, doctore debutante!

FIRST DOCTOR. Cum your kind permissione,
Can I ask him one questione?
We make our pills as white as snow;
What's the reason, do you know?

ARGAN. They have to be bright
To stand out at night.

CHORUS. Bene, bene replicata.
It's clear you've learnt the data.
We'll grant to you the Charter.

SECOND DOCTOR. And next, cum great respect,
How would you expect
To deal with dropsy?

ARGAN. That's easy. Dropsy?
  Enema, khazi, plopsy.

CHORUS. Bene, bene replicata.
  It's clear you've learnt the data.
  We'll grant to you the Charter.

THIRD DOCTOR. If the doctors will permit me,
  I'll ask our learnèd toff
  How he'd deal with a coff.

ARGAN. For anything asthmatic,
  Try an emetic.

CHORUS. Bene, bene replicata.
  It's clear you've learnt the data.
  We'll grant to you the Charter.

FOURTH DOCTOR. One last question, if I may.
  What do you think you'd have to say
  To those malingerers
  Who come to see us
  With breathing dificultates?

ARGAN. For things respiratory,
  Suppository.

FIFTH DOCTOR:What if it endures?

ARGAN. No other cures.
  Don't clean it or wash it or boil it.
  Smile nicely, and point to the toilet.

CHORUS. Bene, bene replicata.
  It's clear you've learnt the data.
  We'll grant to you the Charter.

PRESIDENT. Make sure your great fame runs
    Through every land and border,
    And swear to keep all bums
    In perfect running order.

ARGAN. I swear.

PRESIDENT. The next commandment here is . . .
    Poo-poo the latest theories.

ARGAN. Poo-poo? I will.

PRESIDENT. Never leave them in the lurch
    Till they drop off the perch.

ARGAN. I swear.

PRESIDENT. With this bonnet I thee wed,
    I now pronounce you doctor.
    You have been profoundly
    And venerably doctored.
    By the power of Almighty Medicine,
    You may go forth and medicate,
    Dilate, inflate, berate, truncate, pontificate.
    You may purge, inject, cleanse,
    Bleed, dry and finish off . . .
    Anywhere in the world.
    And ego te absolvo of all responsibilitate!

*Dance. All the surgeons and apothecaries pay their respects,
accompanied by music.*

ARGAN. Doctores of doctoring,
    Royals of flushing,
    Scourges of amnesia,
    Milkmen of magnesia,

By Saint Syrup of Figs, the Puller of Chains,
I'd be daft to pit my brains
Against your massive cerebella.
You're the great light, I'm a dim fellah.
You're the first bright day of Spring,
The sea, the stars, that kind of thing.
All my life I'll be in your debt,
Doctors, the ne plus ultra violet.
Thanks to my pater familias
I have fundamentum gravitas
Ego sum so . . . compost mentis,
But I'll serve as your apprentice.
I am now so allegretto
That my heart sings out falsetto,
I'll wear with pride the gown and cap-o,
I'll be like Doctor Lillicrap-o!

CHORUS. Long live the nova doctor!
    He parley well! A lovely speaker!
    May he eat and drink his fill,
    Bleed, drain, purge, evacuate and kill.
    Three cheers for Dr Argan!
    Take a long deep breath . . .
    Hip, hip, hip, hip, hip hooray!
    Our newest Doctor Death!

Dance. The surgeons and apothecaries dance to the sound of instruments, singing, clapping and apothecaries' mortars.

FIRST SURGEON. May he find the magic cures
    In time-honoured style.
    May he make such a killing
    The banks will be willing
    To sit on his pile.

CHORUS. Long live the nova doctor!
   He parley well! A lovely speaker!
   May he eat and drink his fill,
   Bleed, drain, purge, evacuate and kill.
   Three cheers for Dr Argan!
   Take a long deep breath . . .
   Hip, hip, hip, hip, hip hooray!
   Our newest Doctor Death!

SECOND SURGEON. May he have a succession,
   An endless procession
   Of pox, plague and fever!
   May he drink and be merry,
   Get good dysentery,
   Our Argan, Believer, Reliever!

CHORUS. Long live the nova doctor!
   He parley well! A lovely speaker!
   May he eat and drink his fill,
   Bleed, drain, purge, evacuate and kill.
   May fatal illness cheer him up!
   Raise your glasses, bottoms up!
   A little purge to loosen up!
   Raise your glasses, bottoms up!
   May the hard bowel soften up!
   Raise your glasses, bottoms up!
   The patient's number's coming up!
   Raise your glasses, bottoms up!
   One last drink now, bottoms up!
   Just raise your glasses, BOTTOMS UP!

Final dance. Doctors, surgeons, apothecaries exit by rank with the same ceremony as when they entered.

The End